Arbitration

Money Laundering, Corruption and Fraud

Dossiers - ICC Institute of
World Business Law

Edited by Kristine Karsten
and Andrew Berkeley

The world business organization

Published in September 2003 by

ICC PUBLISHING S.A.
An affiliate of ICC: the world business organization
38, Cours Albert 1er
75008 Paris – France

ICC Publication 651
ISBN 92 842 1320 7

Contents

Foreword

By Serge Lazareff
Chairman, ICC Institute of World Business Law

What a pleasure! At last the Institute is resuming its publications, a tradition successfully established by the ICC Institute's founder, Professor Pierre Lalive. We intend to publish yearly the proceedings of our Annual General Meeting, as well as a second publication, the "best of". We will in our regular programmes – PIDAs and IAAPs – select for publication certain of the papers submitted by our speakers. Of course, all of them are good, but we shall try to offer a range of studies covering topics of interest – particularly current ones.

Our first publication is therefore devoted to our November 2002 Annual General Meeting. "Arbitration, money laundering, corruption and fraud" was approved by the Institute Council as a topic and we decided to set up a working group to study this very delicate question. When the group, led by Andrew W.A. Berkeley and Kristine Karsten, including Bernardo Cremades and Antonio Crivellaro, presented the results of their reflections, the Council found the matter so rich and dense that we all agreed to dedicate the next Annual Meeting, the most prestigious annual event of the Institute, to this matter. Indeed, it would have been a pity not to spread the ideas expressed by this group, as this knowledge and expertise had to be shared and publicized. In addition to these valuable speakers from the group, we decided to call on "external" prestigious experts: Alan Jenkins, Mark Pieth, Giorgio Sacerdoti, Arthur Harverd and Allan Philip. I would like to take this opportunity to thank them all for the remarkable work they did, and the tremendous input they gave to this Annual Meeting.

One of the aims of this conference was to create doctrine, rather than merely to compile information that already existed. We found that the papers and discussions centered around the duty of the arbitrator when money laundering is suspected, the duty of the parties, but also duty to society in general. Laws today tend to implicate lawyers in the reporting of not only offenses which clearly have been committed, but also suspected offenses. This raises the fundamental question of the freedom of the lawyer and of the arbitrator. Is counsel to report somebody coming to him for advice? Is the arbitrator, entrusted with a sacred mission of rendering an award, bound to report a case if he has only a suspicion that something is wrong? These are essential questions in the society of today and I am certain that you will find the answer in the present publication – may I repeat, our first in a long time.

I am convinced it will throw new light on the subject, and hope that every reader will enjoy these pages as much as we enjoyed working on them.

I look forward to meeting all of you, readers and speakers, at our 23rd Annual General Meeting, which will be held on 1 December 2003 in Paris on the topic of "Arbitration and oral evidence."

Contributors

ANDREW W.A. BERKELEY, FCIARB.,

is a Barrister and Arbitrator, Member of the Energy and Utilities Panel of the CPR Institute for Dispute Resolution, New York and First Vice President of the ICC Institute. He was the first Chairman of the International Arbitration Club of London. He has practised as an international commercial arbitrator for ten years, having previously headed three legal departments in major British enterprises in the chemical, oil and gas, and telecommunications industries. He is also a consultant to the Multinationals Group, ICC (UK) and in that capacity has represented British Industry in the negotiation of international trade and investment conventions, including the OECD Convention for Combating the Bribery of Foreign Government Officials.

ROBERT BRINER

is Chairman of the ICC International Court of Arbitration, Paris, and Attorney, Counsel of law, at the law firm Lenz & Staehelin in Geneva. He is Panel Chairman of the United Nations Compensation Commission, former Member of the Claims Resolution Tribunal for Dormant Accounts in Switzerland and former President of the Iran-United States Claims Tribunal in The Hague. He is also former Chair of the Section on Business Law of the International Bar Association (IBA) and Member of the International Council for Commercial Arbitration (ICCA), the International Council of Arbitration for Sport and the Executive Board of the Swiss Arbitration Association. He has written numerous publications, particularly on the subject of arbitration.

BERNARDO CREMADES

is the senior partner of the law firm B. Cremades y Asociados in Madrid, specializing in international commercial arbitration and commercial law. He is President of the Spanish Court of Arbitration, Council Member of the ICC Institute of World Business Law, Chairman of the Global Center for Dispute Resolution Research, and a Member of the International Council for Commercial Arbitration.

ANTONIO CRIVELLARO

is a Council Member of the ICC Institute, Professor of International Trade Law at Padua University, and partner in the law firm Bonelli Erede Pappalardo, Milan office, where he heads the "International Litigation Department". He has extensive experience in international commercial arbitration, especially in the field of construction and investment disputes, either as party's counsel or arbitrator. He has acted and is acting before ICC, ICSID, LCIA, SCC, Cairo Centre of International Commercial Arbitration, Bangkok Arbitration Office, and Milan Chamber of Arbitration.

ARTHUR HARVERD

is a Chartered Accountant and Chartered Arbitrator and is a consultant to Carter Backer Winter, London. As the former head of a panel of independent accountants which assists Scotland Yard's Metropolitan Fraud Squad, he has undertaken many fraud and money laundering investigations and has acted as an expert accountant in several high-profile trials. He now mainly practices as an arbitrator. He is a past Chairman of The Chartered Institute of Arbitrators and is on the Board of Directors of the LCIA and the International Dispute Resolution Centre, London.

ALAN JENKINS

is a partner and head of International at Eversheds, an international law firm. Before his appointment to that position he was a partner in the commercial litigation group. He has extensive experience of transnational litigation and arbitration, involving complex fraud across-borders. His most recent case was the criminal trial involving those accused of the Lockerbie bombing. He is the author of the chapter on investigations in International Commercial Fraud, published by Sweet & Maxwell.

KRISTINE KARSTEN

is a partner of Eversheds Frere Cholmeley, Paris, France, and Council Member of the ICC Institute of World Business Law. She has had broad experience in various fields of corporate law, but is more particularly specialized in banking and financial law, as well as real estate law, in an international environment. In this context, she has acquired a certain familiarity with the techniques used in money laundering operations and commercial fraud and is often called upon to assist banks and businesses in developing and implementing procedures aimed at reducing their exposure to these crimes. A frequent speaker at conferences on the subject, Ms Karsten has also been an active speaker at conferences on other topics organized by ICC.

SERGE LAZAREFF

is a Member of the Paris Bar, partner of Lazareff & Associés. He is Doctor of Law of the University of Paris and holds an LL.M. from Harvard. He is Chairman of the ICC Institute of World Business Law and Chairman of the French Arbitration Commission of ICC, France. He was formerly General Counsel for Inter-national Operations and Vice-President Asia-Pacific of Pechiney, one of the leading French industrial groups.

ALLAN PHILIP

is senior partner, Philip & Partners, Copenhagen, Denmark. He is former Professor at the University of Copenhagen and Dean of the Law School, Member of the Institut de Droit International and of the Curatorium of the Hague Academy of International Law, Chairman of the Panel on Oil Sector Claims in the United Nations' Compensation Commission for the Gulf War, Delegate of Denmark to a number of diplomatic conferences on private international law and maritime law, as well as Member of the Chartered Institute of Arbitrators and the International Arbitration Club of London.

MARK PIETH

is Professor of Criminal Law and Criminology at the University of Basel, Switzerland. He is former Head of Section on Economic and Organised Crime in the Swiss Federal Office of Justice (Ministry of Justice and Police). As an official and later as a consultant to governments, he has acquired extensive experience in international *fora*, most notably as a Member of the Financial Action Task Force on Money Laundering (FATF), the Chemical Action Task Force on Precursor Chemicals, as Chairman of an Intergovernmental Expert Group of the UN to determine the extent of illicit trafficking in drugs and as the Chair of the OECD Working Group on Bribery in International Business Transactions.

GIORGIO SACERDOTI

is an attorney, professor of international law at Bocconi University, Milan, Member of the Appellate Body of the WTO, Geneva, and formerly Vice-Chairman of the OECD Working Group on Bribery in International Business Transactions. He is an expert on international trade and investment law and on the law of international contracts and arbitration. He was a member of the OECD Working Group since its establishment in 1989 until 2001 as a delegate and expert for Italy. He chaired the Group of Experts that prepared the draft of the OECD Convention against Bribery in 1996-97 and was active in the negotiation of the Convention's text.

Introduction

By Kristine Karsten and Andrew Berkeley
Co-editors

This collection of papers results from the proceedings of the 2002 Annual General Meeting of the ICC Institute of World Business Law, held at ICC Headquarters in Paris, on the topic of arbitration in the face of money laundering, corruption and fraud. Ninety-five lawyers, other professionals and businessmen attended to hear the ten speakers and participate in the lively discussion sessions, which showed both the interest and sophistication of the audience. We reproduce here the text of the contributions and a selection of the questions and comments. The Editors and the ICC, as an institution, are most grateful to all of the speakers and participants.

With this publication, the Institute of World Business Law, under the Presidency of Serge Lazareff, resumes its tradition of making available in book form the thinking of its distinguished members and participants on topics of interest and importance in law and business–especially in the international field. In his foreword, Mr. Lazareff says that he hopes that the Institute will have contributed to the formation of "doctrine" on the treatment of corruption, fraud and money laundering in arbitration. Certainly, the editors believe, there are incisive and well considered statements in all of the papers and it may be that there are points of coalescence about arbitration practice when it has to deal with the evils that are the subject of this book. But, this area is rapidly evolving. Indeed, to borrow a phrase from the magisterial paper by Professor Cremades, we in the business and legal worlds are today faced with "a cascade of norms." Laws, treaties, conventions and codes of conduct proliferate. Their authors and promulgators range in skill and learning from the heights of Professor Pieth and Professor Sacerdoti, who were instrumental in the formulation of the influential and successful OECD Convention of 1998, to those who, rather mindlessly, call for "an intensification of the war against corruption" without considering the efficacy of what they propose or its unintended side effects on legitimate enterprise and traditional rights and freedoms. Further evolution of the legal environment being inevitable, it is doubtful that a definitive body of doctrine as to how arbitrators should deal with money laundering, fraud and corruption can yet be settled.

Nonetheless, the ICC Institute can make an important contribution. Since ICC is among the most well-known of international business organizations, its reflections should be based on an objective and thorough examination of the current environment and directed to the efficiency, well-being and integrity of business. Further, since both legislators (domestic and international) and the general world are not well informed about the process of arbitration, the scientific authority of the papers in this collection will, we hope, have a beneficial influence.

It may be of assistance to the reader if we say something about the method adopted in putting together the program on which this book is based. The first part of the program, and thus of this book, is devoted to context. We start with two practicing lawyers, Kristine Karsten and Alan Jenkins, who describe, respectively, the nature of the problems which they and other professionals face and the solutions which they adopt in their daily business. As is clear from their two papers, the activities of money launderers and fraudsters, in particular, are increasingly sophisticated and pernicious and the actions that can and must, in the emerging regulatory environment, be taken by professionals to detect and combat such activities are also increasingly sophisticated.

In this first section, we also present the papers by Professors Pieth and Sacerdoti– eminent criminal law and international law specialists, respectively. Especially interesting is Professor Pieth's conclusion that an international public policy banning bribery is emerging and his challenge, as one of the architects of that new order, to arbitrators about how they are going to reflect it in their practice. He concedes that the decisions will be difficult. Professor Sacerdoti gives a thorough analysis of one of the most highly successful international instruments, the OECD Convention, and ends with suggestions about new areas of activity for the OECD work group, and notably the treatment of foreign subsidiaries and the working of offshore financial centers, which are of relevance to many international arbitrations.

In the second part, we concentrate directly on the problems raised for arbitrators by money laundering, fraud and bribery. The section opens with a significant paper by Bernardo Cremades and David Cairns. Drawing on Professor Cremades' immense experience and deep thought, the analysis represents the most complete acceptance, so far, from within the arbitration community that there now exists a normative international public policy, binding on arbitrators, to address issues of bribery, money laundering and serious fraud whenever they arise. Professor Cremades frankly acknowledges that the position he advocates is likely to raise delicate practical difficulties.

It is agreed by everyone who has encountered money laundering, fraud or corruption in an arbitration that the relevant issue is often one of evidence. Arthur Harverd, an accountant, contributes a paper on the role of the expert as witness and investigator. There then follows a monumental investigation by Professor Crivellaro of the reported arbitration cases where fraud and corruption have featured. We think that the record there established will be of use to all future scholars in the field. Finally, we have the subtle and balanced paper by Professor Alan Phillip, the main theme of which is the question of whether an arbitrator, by investigating fraud or corruption issues, not explicitly raised by the parties, may be in danger of making findings *ultra petita*. He draws on the relevant analogy of cases where anti-trust considerations may apply.

We have not been able to include all of the comments made by the audience from the floor during the question and discussion sessions, but we have printed a selection, grouping them generally under topics raised by the speakers. Especially noteworthy is the comment by Robert Briner, President of the ICC International Court of Arbitration, who drew many of the threads together.

Have we then fulfilled Serge Lazareff's hope that the Meeting would establish a body of doctrine? Perhaps not yet, but we believe that the Institute, in this thought-provoking initiative, has identified some elements which will, undoubtedly, contribute to the formation of such a body in the course of time.

1

Money laundering:
How it works and why you should be concerned

By Kristine Karsten
Partner, Eversheds Frere Cholmeley, Paris, France;
Council Member, ICC Institute of World Business Law

1.   MONEY LAUNDERING: THE NUMBERS

Money laundering is, and has been for several years now, a subject that is very much in the public eye? Why?

Well, to start with, it is a subject that affects a substantial portion of the world economy. How substantial? Estimates vary considerably, but concur on one point: the sums involved are considerable and, worse, growing. The International Monetary Fund, for example, estimates that the annual "turnover" of money laundering is between 2 and 5% of the worldwide gross domestic product (between 600 billion and 1.5 trillion US dollars)[1]. By way of compari-son, the gross domestic product of a country like Spain is only roughly 590 billion US dollars[2]. In France alone, the estimated volume of funds laundered locally per year is 6 billion Euros, for a total of some 130 billion of criminal-origin funds that may already have been injected into the French economy (1/2 of all foreign investments)[3]!

As for the growth of the phenomenon, it can be attributed to a number of factors. First, as the French numbers suggest, the principle is that "once dirty, always dirty." Thus, the various estimates take into account not only the fresh proceeds of criminal activities being injected yearly into the legitimate economy, but also the cumulative total of past injections and the profits generated by them. Second, money launderers and the criminals who employ them are increasingly sophisticated. The fortunes at their command give them access to high-quality accounting, tax and legal advice (both from unscrupulous professionals and from professionals who simply fail—out of incompetence or inexperience or because they are being deliberately deceived by their clients—to recognize the true nature of the transaction). Third, international movements of funds are increasingly fluid, thanks notably to innovations in the financial and quasi-financial products market, technological advances such as the generalization of secure financial transactions via the Internet and the legislative abolition or reduction of exchange control or direct investment regulations in many countries. And finally, the definition of money laundering has expanded to sweep in a much broader range of activities.

2.   A FEW DEFINITIONS

How, exactly, is money laundering defined? The precise legal definition of money laundering varies from one country to another and may, within a single country, have several definitions (for example, the definition provided in the Penal Code or equivalent text and that used in banking or other regulatory texts or in recommendations issued by professional organizations). The common denominator is that money laundering always designates the processing of "criminal proceeds" to disguise their illegal origin.

As to the activities that may give rise to "criminal proceeds," the list is not the same from country to country nor from year to year and depends on what is characterized as a "crime": drug trafficking, certainly, and racketeering or prostitution, but also, today, terrorism, arms sales and also, sometimes, tax fraud.

As for the processing, it may take, as we will see, many forms, but is universally aimed at permitting criminals to enjoy and continue to control the fruits of their illegal activities, without jeopardizing the source. The objective pursued in a money laundering operation is thus very different from that in a fraudulent transaction or one involving corruption. Indeed, the purpose of a fraud is to create a profit, not to disguise one. And the purpose of corruption is to procure a benefit by giving funds to a third party, not to retain the use of the funds.

3.   THE MONEY LAUNDERING PROCESS

Money laundering is generally described as a three-step process, using the services of bankers, lawyers, accountants and other professionals and, in many cases, benefiting from the protection offered by legislation in "friendly" countries.

The first of the three steps in money laundering is the phase colorfully called "smurfing" (a term intended to evoke the involvement or a large number of individuals who are relatively lowly members of the criminal organization). During this phase, cash is converted, through a succession of small and, to the extent possible, anonymous transactions, into a bank deposit or other negotiable, redeemable or saleable instrument or object. The archetypal example of "smurfing" would be that of a bank account opened in the name of a corporation, into which a series of individuals make, repeatedly, cash deposits that are, individually, sufficiently small to fall below the declaratory threshold for the bank in question. A slightly more complex example is that of a series of individuals who remit travelers' checks or wire funds, paid for in cash, to a single recipient abroad. In all of these cases, cash of dubious origins is placed in the banking system, from which it can subsequently be withdrawn in a form that does not readily reveal those origins.

The second and third phases are called, more prosaically, layering (that is, converting or moving the funds to distance them from their source) and integration (that is, injecting the funds into the legitimate economy). An example of layering would be using a bank account that is opened and funded by cash deposits to buy, preferably in another country, a luxury car that is then sold in exchange for a check from a legitimate buyer. An example of integration would be to use the proceeds from that check to buy machines for, say, a ... laundromat[4].

From this brief description of the money laundering process, it is clear that the services of professional advisers are required by money launderers, at a minimum, to create the corporation into which the illicit funds are ultimately "integrated." More commonly, money launderers (and, more to the point, the principals they represent) act like the very rich people they are and seek out competent legal, tax, financial and accounting advice not only in order to cloak their transactions in an air of legitimacy, but also to minimize taxes, limit on-going operating expenses and recurrent overhead and maximize profits or resale value.

Another by-product of the fact that money launderers (and their principals) are very rich is that the legislation in numerous countries has been slow to integrate anti-money laundering provisions. These countries include the home territories of certain drug traffickers (for example, Guatemala) or other criminal organizations (for example, Ukraine). They also include developing countries with little incentive to cooperate in international cross-border policing activities (for example, Nigeria) and, traditionally, countries with few natural resources that have achieved international prominence by offering to domicile, with few formalities and no taxes, local "off-the-shelf" corporations, including in many instances banks.

A "blacklist" of the countries deemed to be friendly to money launderers is published from time to time by the Financial Action Task Force on money laundering ("FATF" or, in French, "GAFI"[5]), a multi-country[6] organization set up, in 1989, at the G-7 Summit held in Paris, for the purpose of "examining money laundering techniques and trends, reviewing the action which had already been taken at a national or international level, and setting out the measures that still needed to be taken to combat money laundering.[7]" Surprisingly, perhaps, this so-called "blacklist" does not include, or more precisely no longer includes, a certain number of countries that top the list of countries commonly perceived as tax havens – the Cayman Islands, the Bahamas and Liechtenstein, notably – or that are reputed to be the "home turf" of criminal organizations of international importance – Panama and Russia, for example. These seeming omissions are due to the fact that the countries in question have at long last, often after considerable vacillation, adopted stringent anti-money laundering laws, which they seem to be enforcing.

4. EXAMPLES OF MONEY LAUNDERING SCHEMES

How, exactly, is money laundered? The methods used by money launderers are varied and, often, complex. For the purposes of illustration, however, let us focus briefly on five examples of money laundering transactions.

Given the topic under consideration today – money laundering (and fraud and corruption) and arbitration – the first example, appropriately, is that of using judicial or arbitral proceedings to legitimate a payment. How does it work? Very simply: a complicit but apparently unrelated party in Country X asserts a spurious or inflated claim against a party in Country Y seeking to move large amounts of cash into Country X. The defendant (or respondent) then contrives to lose the action and makes payment of the judgment or award entered against it using cash or thinly-disguised proceeds of criminal activity (for example, the balance of a bank account created using cash deposits).

And *voilà*, the plaintiff (or claimant), which in reality is controlled by or acting for the same principals as the defendant (or respondent), acquires a significant amount of cash (which in many countries is considered as a tax-free income) that it can easily explain to its banker and the tax authorities, and the defendant has, potentially, a loss that it can set off against its local tax obligations.

What is undoubtedly a far more common money laundering scheme is that in which a money launderer undertakes to buy an asset (such as real estate or a business) and offers, as security for the payment of the price, a pledge over an offshore collateral account (that is, a bank deposit containing cash of dubious origin). When, surprise of surprises, the money launderer defaults, the seller is paid using the bank deposit and the money launderer acquires a valuable asset that he can then sell on to a third party for funds that are much easier to account for than was the original cash.

Import-export sales are also easy vectors for money laundering. All you need do is have excess, and illicit-origin, cash in one country that is used to buy overpriced goods in another country, using and abusing, for this purpose, a standard letter of credit structure[8]. The seller then has income that it can explain without difficulty; the buyer has goods that it can resell for a "legitimate" profit. The two parties need not be related. Indeed, for many sellers, the incentive of being able to sell goods at above the prevailing market price is sufficient incentive to justify turning a blind eye to the probable origin of the funds used to pay their invoices. Moreover, for money laundering buyers, a transaction cost of up to 20% or more (in the form of a difference between the purchase price of the goods and the amount for which they can be resold, plus expenses) may be perfectly acceptable[9], if the result is to make the net funds available for reinvestment without attracting unwanted official attention.

A somewhat more colorful example is that of the Parisian "Asian ants." A few years ago, the Paris police uncovered an Asian money laundering gang working in Paris. The gang recruited, from local Asian neighborhoods, individuals who were, daily, given illegal-origin cash in a pre-agreed amount and asked to impersonate Japanese or other oriental tourists and buy, for cash, luxury goods such as Vuitton handbags and Dior scarves, which they handed over the same day to the gang. The gang then boxed the goods and shipped them to buyers in the Middle East and Asia. To be sure, the resale netted less than the cash expended, but the indirect profit – in terms of illegal cash that transformed into easily explainable checks for goods sold – was considerable.

Yet another example is that of sales contracts where the goods (or, for example, products like insurance policies) are purchased by the money launderer either by paying several cash installments, each of which is below any reporting threshold applicable to cash payments, or by paying in kind. Before the final payment is made, the money launderer terminates the contract and obtains reimbursement, by check from the seller, of the sums paid to date.

Of course, now that money laundering is considered in certain countries to include investments made using the gains from tax fraud[10], money laundering may take the form, for example, of a merchant endorsing checks received by him from his customers over to an offshore company or, where checks cannot be endorsed[11], accepting checks with the identity of the payee left in blank in payment and inserting the name of the offshore company as payee. In such cases, the merchant is presumably under-declaring his income, since the checks remitted to the offshore company do not transit through his bank account. The merchant will ultimately recover the funds paid by him either because he holds an interest in the offshore company (which may be required to pay tax on its "income," but undoubtedly at a far lower rate, due to its location in a low-tax jurisdiction) or because the offshore company uses part or all of the money to purchase assets, also offshore, for the account of the merchant.

5. RISK FACTORS

The underlying principle of most current laws on money laundering is that, notwithstanding the variety of techniques used by money launderers, there are a certain number of factors that should, almost as a matter of course, elicit suspicion in an alert banker or other professional.

First among these is the involvement, particularly if for no apparent purpose, of transfers of funds from or to a "blacklisted" country. Today, only eleven of these "blacklisted" countries remain: the Cook Islands, Egypt, Grenada, Guatemala, Indonesia, Myanmar, Nauru, Nigeria, the Philippines, Saint Vincent and the Grenadines, and Ukraine. Many bankers, however, continue to include on their personal watch lists countries removed only recently, or due to intense political pressure, from the FAFT list. Thus, for example, financial transactions with countries such as the Cayman Islands, Israel or Russia continue to be scrutinized closely by many banks.

Countries appearing on the past and present FATF "blacklists" are, of course, not the only countries that, in practice, are treated with a certain suspicion. In particular, a certain number of countries, considered as a likely home for funds and companies belonging to money launderers because they constitute financial havens, are often included by banks, for example, on their internal watch lists. What are the characteristics of financial havens? Generally, they have no tax treaties providing for the sharing of information with other countries or are lax in enforcing information-sharing provisions. Generally, too, they offer inexpensive "off-the-shelf" corporations and enforce strict standards of confidentiality in banking and corporate matters. In many cases, they also have an excellent infrastructure for electronic communications, use a major world currency, and preferably the United States dollar, as local money and benefit from a local government that is relatively invulnerable to outside pressure. They may also have a large tourist trade that can help explain major inflows of cash and a geographic location facilitating business travel to and from rich neighbors. Finally, they frequently have a well-developed, internationally savvy, financial services sector that generates a significant amount of local income.

Other characteristics of a transaction, above and beyond the countries involved in it, are also deemed to warrant, inherently, greater scrutiny. Thus, for example, certain professions are generally considered, with a certain amount of justification, to be particularly susceptible to use as a conduit for money laundering. Banks, of course, were the first conscripts in the war against money laundering on the very logical basis that the initial step in any money laundering scheme – smurfing – consists of injecting the liquid proceeds of crime into the banking system and the second step – layering – generally consists of moving the funds, for the most part through banking channels, to another location or account. As a result, banks are, in many countries[12], required to put in place internal control procedures directly aimed at identifying suspected cases of money laundering and reporting them to the relevant authorities, the bank's duty of confidentiality to its customers being superseded, in such cases, by the bank's reporting obligation.

Other professions have since been added, in many countries, to the initial list of professions that are obligated by law[13] to report any suspected money laundering of which they may become aware. These professions are those deemed to be particularly susceptible to use by money launderers to transform cash into goods that can be easily resold or returned in exchange for a check.

Antiques dealers and dealers in precious stones or artwork are an obvious example. They frequently accept cash from their customers and their goods are often easy to transport and have an intrinsic value that permits resale locally or in another country without excessive difficulty or risk of loss.

A slightly less obvious, but arguably more significant, vector for money laundering is that of real estate sales. Typically, money laundering in this sector takes the form of a purchase agreement in which part of the price is either undisclosed or disguised as a commission or payment for furnishings, for example, and is paid offshore and, if possible, in cash. For the seller, this arrangement makes it possible to limit capital gains taxes. For the buyer, the part of the price paid in cash will be recovered when the property is resold for what is ostensibly a "profit." In the case of luxury properties, in particular, this type of manipulation may be difficult to identify, since numerous factors – the financial situation of the seller, the attachment of the buyer to the property or work carried out between the first and second transactions[14,] for example – may quite legitimately cause the price of a given property to vary from one sale to another, even within a relatively brief lapse of time. Because of the propensity of money launderers to use real estate sales to convert cash into apparently legitimate-source income, real estate brokers were among the professionals specifically subjected by existing international legislation to an obligation of increased vigilence.

Not all sectors that are in fact used by money launderers as conduits for converting cash into goods or investments are included on the various legislative lists of professions subject to a specific reporting obligation. For example, import-export sales may, as noted above, also be used by money launderers to move money from one country to another and laundromats (and restaurants) are also popular investments for money launderers, due to the fact that they generate cash that can be explained when depositing it in the bank. Nonetheless, these professions are in most countries not currently subjected to a specific reporting requirement.

Car, truck and motorcycle dealerships, which are now subject to a reporting requirement in the US[15] but for the most part not elsewhere, are another example of a vector favored by money launderers that has, until now, been subjected to only limited regulatory control. For a money launderer, a car, motorcycle or truck, if it can be purchased wholly or in part for cash and resold to a legitimate purchaser for a check, permits more cash to be converted in a single operation than does, for example, the sale of a Vuitton handbag. Moreover, most motor vehicles have a readily ascertainable value (a very useful attribute from the money launderer's perspective) and are, by definition, mobile and can easily be resold at a certain distance from their point of purchase (yet another valuable attribute). As an added bonus, for the money launderer, between purchase and sale a luxury car can be used by the money launderer for his personal purposes.

Although the businesses that are popular with money launderers are far too legion to be listed in a brief discussion of the phenomenon (remember that we are speaking, roughly, of a trillion dollar per year market), one final sector merits special mention: the market for consultancy and other professional services, particularly in transactions with financial havens[16]. Here, the money launderer's objective is not to acquire goods with a specific resale value, nor to add value to property that can be recovered on disposal of the property, but to structure international investments and movements of funds so as to attract the least official attention, minimize taxes (but not avoid them, since paying taxes lends an air of legitimacy to the transaction) and reduce operating costs. For the professional, these objectives may appear to be, and indeed are, perfectly consistent with those of a legitimate businessman. Moreover, the ostensible purpose of the transaction – facilitating the purchase of a luxury property in France, for example – may also appear wholly legitimate. Nonetheless, like bankers, professionals specialized in "tax optimization" cross-border transactions are likely to be, wittingly or not, occasionally or more regularly, at the heart of a certain number of money laundering transactions. It is for this reason that, increasingly, professional advisors are among those singled out as having certain reporting obligations under money laundering laws[17].

Finally, existing money laundering laws also identify, as flags marking potential money laundering activities, manifestly overpriced or underpriced transactions (because they generate unequal flows of funds or goods not easily explainable by ordinary commercial objectives), transactions of unusual complexity or dubious profitability (because the need to distance cash from its source may, for a money launderer, impose structuring considerations that outweigh the desire to earn a profit on the transactions) and transactions involving unusual or exotic sources of funding (again, due to the need to convert illicit-origin offshore cash or assets previously purchased using illicit-origin cash into what appears to be a legitimate investment).

All of the foregoing risk factors are taken into account in at least some of the existing anti-money laundering laws.

6.   WHAT ARE THE PRIMARY APPLICABLE LAWS?

Internationally, several layers of texts may apply. While the United States enacted domestic legislation directed at identifying money laundering activities as early as 1970 (the date of the United States Bank Secrecy Act requiring cash transactions over a certain threshold to be declared by banks), the first international initiatives of significance were taken in Europe. Indeed, in 1980, the Council of Europe issued Recommendations on money laundering. It was almost ten years later, however, before the first concrete measures were adopted and regional conventions were concluded, initially in Europe only, to take concerted action against money launderers.

Thus, in 1989, at a European Summit (held two years after the enactment, in the United States once again, of the Money Laundering Control Act), it was decided to create the FATF. Shortly after its creation, the FATF issued a list of forty recommendations for identifying and attacking suspected money laundering transactions. These recommendations, with modifications, have largely inspired the international conventions and national legislation subsequently enacted to address money laundering issues.

The first truly international convention to be adopted was the Council of Europe's Convention on Laundering, Search, Seizure and Confiscation of the Proceeds of Crime, signed in Strasbourg, France, on November 8, 1990[18]. It was followed almost immediately by the first European directive on the subject, EC Directive 91/308 of June 10, 1991, on the prevention of the use of the financial system for the purpose of money laundering. In recent years, there has been a flurry of international treaties or conventions on the subject of money laundering: the Model Regulations Concerning the Laundering Offences Connected to Illicit Drug Trafficking and Other Serious Offences enacted by the Organization of the American States in 1998, the International Convention for the Suppression of Terrorism enacted on December 9, 1999, the Model Legislation on Laundering, Confiscation and International Co-operation in Relation to the Proceeds of Crime (for civil law jurisdictions) enacted in Vienna in 1999, the corresponding Vienna convention, enacted in 2000, for common law jurisdictions (the Model Money Laundering and Proceeds of Crime Bill) and the EC Directive 2001/97 of December 4, 2001, amending EC Directive 91/308.

Throughout the world, local money laundering laws have been adopted, particularly in the past decade. Indeed, the FATF, which for many years has issued lengthy lists of those "non-cooperative countries and territories" (the so-called "blacklist") whose anti-money laundering legislation and local enforcement efforts were judged insufficient, has recently reduced its list, as noted above, to a mere eleven countries.

Local legislation varies, of course. Traditionally, money laundering legislation followed one of two models: the United States model or the European model. In the United States, where, as noted above, the first legislative texts are now over thirty years old, the initial approach was to require banks to report automatically all cash transactions in excess of a certain amount, whether or not they appeared suspicious. In Europe, the approach was to require banks (and, for the past ten years, certain other professionals such as real estate brokers) to get to know their customers and identify and declare suspicious transactions only. Today, the two approaches have largely converged. In the USA Patriot Act 2001, numerous professionals, and not just bankers, are now required to take concrete steps to confirm the identity of their customers and to scrutinize and declare transactions that appear suspicious. Under the most recent EC Directive, which is currently being implemented into local law in European countries, the traditional know-your-customer rules continue to apply, but automatic declarations must now be made in certain cases, even in the absence of suspicions.

French legislation is a good illustration of the modern trend in anti-money laundering legislation. The first specific national legislation on the subject of money laundering was enacted in July 1990 and imposed a duty on financial institutions and a limited list of other professionals to declare suspicious activities and created specific, more stringent, obligations for financial institutions alone, which were required to put in place concrete measures to ensure a constant level of vigilance. It was only in May 1996 that money laundering became a specifically identified criminal offense in France and, initially, was tied specifically to the proceeds of drug trafficking and other organized crime. Aiding and abetting money laundering (like revealing the existence of a declaration of suspicious activities to a suspected money launderer) was also made a criminal offence (subject to sanctions even more severe than those applicable to the money launderers themselves). In May 2001, the definition of money laundering was expanded to include the proceeds of any major crime or "organized" criminal activity, a definition that is generally considered to cover tax fraud. Moreover, the obligation to declare suspicious activities was expanded to include automatic declarations in a certain number of cases and to include transactions that "might" involve money laundering (as opposed to the previous standard, that is, transactions that "appear to" involve money laundering). Currently, legislation is being prepared to enact into French domestic law the innovations reflected in the most recent EC Directive, such as the expansion of the list of professions subject to the obligation to declare suspicious activities and the enlargement of the definition of money laundering to include new types of criminal activities.

On top of this legislation, banks and other financial institutions are subject, under the rules issued by the local French banking authorities, to very detailed and comprehensive internal control requirements, including anti-money laun-dering measures. While these regulations have yet to be emulated by other regulatory bodies, such as that responsible for supervising the insurance industry, numerous white papers or guidelines have been issued, both by such bodies and by professional associations. Increasingly, it seems clear, the trend will be to impose on all professionals that are likely to be touched by money laundering activities an active duty of co-operation, inspired at least in part by the obligations already imposed on bankers.

Anti-money laundering legislation is thus evolving rapidly. Most countries are now participating in the fight against money laundering. The definition of what constitutes money laundering has expanded, distancing it from the limited initial arena of organized crime and drug-related offenses to include a broad range of crimes judged, locally at least, "serious." Passive assistance to money launderers is being criminalized. The types of professionals enlisted in the fight against money laundering have been extended from the initial, restrictive, list consisting largely of financial institutions and professionals in the sectors judged to be the most favored among money launderers, such as real estate sales, to include lawyers, accountants and numerous other professionals and, even, in the United States, car salesmen. The duty to obtain proof of customers' identities and to scrutinize transactions has been refined and extended. Automatic declarations in certain cases are becoming obligatory.

The future, clearly, is one of increased regulation.

To form a better idea of the current state of anti-money laundering initiatives, certain web sites can be consulted. In particular:

- Council of Europe: http://conventions.coe.int
- European Union: www.europa.eu.int
- FATF: www.fatf-gafi.org
- Federal Bureau of Investigation: http://www.fbi.gov/hq/cid/fc/ml/ml.htm
- French Finance Ministry: www.finances.gouv.fr
- French Ministry of Interior Affairs:
  http://www.interieur.gouv.fr/police/dcpj/sdaef/Missions.htm
- ICC Commercial Crime Services: http://www. icc-ccs.org
- International Monetary Fund: www.imf.org
- International Money Laundering Information Network:
  http://www.imolin.org
- Interpol: www.interpol.int
- OECD: www.ocde.org
- UN: http://www.un.org and www.undcp.org
- United Kingdom Financial Services Authority: http://www.fsa.gov.uk
- US Treasury Department: www.ustreas.org

FOOTNOTES

1   The International Monetary Fund (www.imf.org).

2   World Bank (www.worldbank.org).

3   French *Assemblée Nationale* (www.assemblee-nat.fr).

4   Laundromats are, as it happens, a popular type of investment for would-be money launderers, since they generate, quite legitimately, cash, and banks holding accounts for laundromats naturally expect to receive deposits in the form of cash and may not be in a position to judge whether the amount of the deposits remitted to them is commensurate with the size and activity of their client's official business. Similar types of businesses that are popular with money launderers are restaurants (pizzerias, for example) and car washes, although any business with a high percentage of cash sales will serve the purpose.

5   Groupement d'Action Financière sur le blanchiment des capitaux.

6   Initially, the Task Force was comprised of members from the G-7 Member States, the European Commission and eight other countries. Today, membership has expanded from the initial 16 members to a total of 28.

7   "History of the FATF" section of the FATF web site, at www.fatf-gafi.org.

8   The buyer opens a letter of credit, secured by a cash deposit, with his bank, which notifies it to the seller's bank. On presentation of the letter of credit, the money lanuderer/buyer's bank transfers funds to the seller's bank, using the cash deposit.

9   Reputedly, however, the transaction cost that is deemed acceptable by today's sophisticated money launderers has declined considerably and is currently significantly below 10%.

10 For example, French money laundering regulations treat tax fraud as being among the illegal activities whose proceeds can be "laundered."

11 Many European countries prohibit the endorsement of checks unless a special form of check is obtained from the bank.

12 All EU countries and the United States, notably.

13 Antiques dealers, insurance companies, currency exchanges and real estate agents, notably.

14 Construction work is another area that offers interesting opportunities for money launderers. Indeed, many small contractors are often quite happy to work for cash. As for the money launderer, the cash outlay is converted into extra value of the property, which will ultimately be resold for an amount taking into the increase in value.

15 Patriot Act 2001, Section 326, and US Code Section 5312 (a) (2).

16 Consultancy in export sales is perhaps not an issue for money laundering purposes, but is often relevant in cases of corruption.

17 Legal and tax advisors, lawyers, accountants, clerks, real estate agent, notably.

18 In the same year, the United States enacted the Depositary Institution Money Laundering Amendment Act.

2

Money laundering, corruption and fraud:
The approach of an international law firm

By Alan Jenkins
International Director, Eversheds, London, United Kingdom

INTRODUCTION

The first point I would make is that this is there is not any single solution to the problems posed by cross-border business crime. The approach is necessarily based on experience of previous cases and adapting techniques to new facts and circumstances. Why is this? It is because however global business is becoming and however much criminals disregard national and state boundaries, the law is still local in its jurisdictional effect and application. This is a trend and a limitation emphasised by the advent of the Internet and its widespread use. It is a feature that exists despite limited exceptions, such as the attempts at concertation within the EU and the muscular exercise in some circumstances of "long arm" jurisdiction by various nations including, for example, the US. This is a problem for national authorities trying to fight the spread of money laundering, corruption and fraud. It has been given new urgency by the war on terror.

At the state level, these concerns have led to the establishment of a number of initiatives. The G-8 group of economic powers has set up a senior experts' group on Transnational Organised Crime. The Council of Europe has issued a draft convention on crime in cyberspace. It is interesting that states which are not members of the Council, such as the US, Canada, South Africa and Japan, have participated in the work of preparation. The European Union has been active too as it seeks to bring together the efforts of the member states, for example in the *Corpus Juris* proposals. The UN Convention on Transnational Organised Crime of 15 December 2000 requires member states to ensure that their domestic laws are adequate to combat organised crime. In the United Kingdom, the

Government and various other agencies, such as the Serious Fraud Office and the Law Commission, are concerned about the effectiveness of our laws, the resources available to the police and prosecutors and the ability of our courts to cope with the increasing incidence of business crime.

What does this mean, therefore, for an international law firm such as mine, asked to advise and assist a client that is the victim of business crime on an international scale? In discussing this I shall focus for the sake of simplicity on the victims of fraud, but the issues are similar whatever form the business crime takes. The civil law and those working in it have none of the coercive powers available to state agencies, even if those are presently regarded as inadequate. What cannot be achieved by voluntary co-operation can only be obtained very often by long and expensive proceedings in court.

1. AWARENESS

We begin with awareness of the implications internally, amongst our lawyers and other members of staff. This involves training and education in the relevant law. That much is obvious. It is important to extend this however to the sharing of practical knowledge and experience with clients, regulators, the police and private investigators who have case studies to share. In addition, in a firm such as mine, which does not have, nor wish to have, a specialist criminal law expertise and practice, it helps to have good relations with firms that do. Such relationships are helpful for the same purpose and also in having readily available expert help on those occasions when a client's needs are such that they require a different sort of specialist help.

Awareness also involves the education of clients. The subject of this paper is not always one that excites clients. Nor is it one that many feel is relevant to them – in the same way that some dreadful illnesses always happen to other people. Yet the statistics are truly alarming. According to a European Commission report of July 1998, US $3 billion was being lost each year as a result of credit card fraud.

Fraud is reported to cost the UK £14 billion per year. History shows that these sorts of business crime can strike even the most reputable and apparently well run businesses – for example Enron, and Barings, the famous British bank that disappeared a few years ago.

Our experience is that too many clients have little or no knowledge of the issues;

they demonstrate a lack of sophistication in dealing with these problems and their reactions to emerging problems are often ones of shock, shame and horror that such things could happen to them.

Against this background, a law firm must demonstrate understanding, sympathy, discretion and the ability to advise and act decisively.

2. THE ENDLESS VARIETIES

Fraud, corruption and money laundering are often hard to recognise. Part of the problem is that to be successful they have to appear as normal, justifiable, plausible transactions. Another part of the problem is that they take many different forms. Whilst there are certain basic types which are repeated again and again, the clever criminal will evolve new schemes to try to hinder detection. I will give three examples of each type of business crime that I have come across recently, just to have them in mind as we go through the topics covered later in this paper. Some of them overlap.

- **Money laundering**: a company placed a contract to buy currency at a future date at a favourable rate and on favourable terms; it transferred £5 million to the dealer's account, but at the appointed date, no foreign currency was forthcoming. Upon taking this up with the management of the dealer company, a variety of excuses were given. Eventually, and under a lot of pressure, the £5 million was repaid in instalments. On investigation, it appeared that the managing director of the dealer spent a great deal of time in Ukraine. He said that it was because he was providing advice to the government of that country on the banking system. Why such a government would turn to an obscure foreign exchange dealer was never clear. It appeared that he might have links to mafia elements. The matter was reported by the company to the British National Criminal Intelligence Service, which subsequently moved in on the dealer and made various arrests. This case was also a fraud in that the client, whilst successful in recovering its capital, was deprived of the use of its money for several months without recompense.

- **Corruption:** a multi-national company does a great deal of business in countries in Asia. It is the custom in many places for gifts to be offered, and indeed expected, as part of the building of a relationship. When is a gift a bribe or an inducement to do business which would not otherwise be done? On the other hand, to refuse a gift or not make one when it is customary in the local culture to do so can ruin a good prospect. In one case, a handsome watch worth many hundreds of pounds was offered to a senior executive. The solution the company adopted was to tell him to accept, to sell the watch and donate the proceeds to charity all in an open way. To avoid embarrassment in the future, as he would clearly not be wearing the watch when he met the giver, he was transferred elsewhere at an early opportunity. It is not always easy or sensible to do this and the solution here is not a good one, but these are very difficult questions. With the advent of new laws, mirroring the US Foreign Trade Corrupt Practices Act and implementing the OECD Anti Bribery Convention, this is an acute area for international business.

- **Fraud:** booking fictitious transactions: I have seen this done in banks, insurance, computer leasing, and the fertiliser industry, amongst others.

An alarming new source of financial crime is the Internet. It is estimated that worldwide trade over the Internet will be worth more than US $1.3 billion by 2004. In that context, it is frightening that gullible people will do things that they would not do otherwise. For example, I came across the case of a US online bank whose customers received an email telling them that the bank had had some problems with their records. The email asked the customers to reply with details of their accounts by re-registering. It provided a link, which was very similar to the bank's. Of course, it was not the bank's, but 250,000 people still re-registered and lost money.

3.   ROLE OF INTERNATIONAL LAW FIRMS

It is necessary to begin by the resources required.

Lawyers experienced in these matters must be available at the client's "home" office. They should be experienced not only in the law and its application to the issues, but also in how to work with the domestic authorities. The police, prosecutors and regulators have different interests amongst themselves and certainly to the client, but co-operation with them can often be useful. To have a difficult relationship with them can often be very damaging.

Such lawyers should also be experienced in knowing that things are different abroad. I will touch on some points later, but it is very easy to think and act as if things must be done the same way abroad as they are at home. If one is faced with a multi-national fraud and a multi-jurisdictional investigation, a keen sense of what needs to be done and by whom is essential.

This leads to the need for a reliable network overseas of lawyers and investigators. The lawyers should be capable of assisting with the civil, criminal and regulatory issues arising. In some countries these are more or less dealt with by one or two bodies; in other countries, for example, the US, there can be a multiplicity of agencies involved at the federal and state level and lawyers experienced in finding a way through the maze are a must.

Lawyers are not all, however.

Today, much business crime is a highly involved and sophisticated affair. Investigators are essential to obtain information, trace witnesses, find assets and generally help with gathering facts and evidence. They come in many different guises, ranging from large multinational organisations like Kroll or Control Risks to one or two person firms. Whatever choice is appropriate in terms of size, one element is essential: they should be people of integrity who will only operate within the law and do what it is proper.

Experts in any number of different fields may be necessary. IT specialists are often required to examine computers and obtain information from them which the suspect had sought to delete but may have done so unsuccessfully. Accountants may be required to help with the accounting trail of suspicious transactions. An expert may be required in the practices of an industry to help gain an understanding of why certain things are done or not done; and so the list goes on.

An international law firm needs to be aware of risks involved. There are two significant areas of risk to bear in mind. The first is that of personal safety. I refer not to threats of violence from criminals, but to the need to observe the law in countries where inquiries are to be made. For example, in Switzerland it is against the law, so I have several times been advised, for a foreign lawyer to enter that country and interview prospective witnesses. That is regarded as being exclusively a matter for the police and judicial authorities. There are ways around this with a willing witness or informant – basically it involves him or her travelling outside Switzerland to be interviewed. If the person is unwilling, then it may be necessary to seek the help of the courts through letters of request under the Hague Convention. In many countries that is a less than perfect solution, because even if the courts will help, it is often not possible to ask questions other than those set out in the request. Even where it is possible to ask more than this, the topics are usually limited to those specified and it is difficult to go into areas that arise unexpectedly.

The second area of risk arises from the need to check that a law firm abroad is in a position to help and does not have a conflict of interest. In providing the information that the foreign firm needs to confirm this, the risk is run that it is indeed acting for the person the subject of the inquiry who may then be tipped off about what is happening. If that happens, he might be able further to cover his tracks. There is not much that can be done about this. In many parts of the world, where lawyers are plentiful it is unlikely to be a major risk. In small states, where there are only a small number of lawyers, the risks are considerably greater. Indeed, these are more than proportionately increased in cases of sophisticated business crime. In such instances, the criminals may have used vehicles in so-called offshore locations and retained local lawyers to set them up and run them. For example, some years ago I was involved in a big insurance fraud case in the City of London, in which premiums had been siphoned out of a well known group of insurance companies to the benefit of a small number of senior executives. The vehicles used were companies set up in countries like Bermudas, sheltered behind Anstalts set up and run in Liechtenstein. In such circumstances, caution is required in approaching law firms in small places to ensure that they have no links to those under investigation.

4. OBJECTIVES

In setting out to help clients who have suffered from one of the forms of business crime, a lawyer needs to know what objectives his client has in mind. This will vary from client to client. It is often the recovery of compensation. Equally important for many is the protection of reputation and the integrity of the brand. For others it might be to know what has happened in order to learn the lessons and put in place new procedures and policies to prevent a recurrence. For some it will be a combination of all of these, and maybe other considerations will play a part too.

If the objective is to recover compensation, how far is the client prepared to go? Does the client want a quick settlement? Is it prepared to go all the way to trial and judgement? Many are the times when in the heat of the moment clients say things like "It doesn't matter how much it costs". Yet after a few months or even years, and after the expenditure of tens, if not hundreds of thousands of pounds, senior executives begin to have second thoughts. Although it is not the easiest time to do so, it is important at an early point to help a client understand what is going to be involved in dealing with a major piece of business crime. It is not just the financial cost involved, but also the commitment of time and attention on the part of senior management and directors, the disruption to the normal business and duties of colleagues in the company and the risk of claims and counterclaims of responsibility – passing the buck. It is worth noting here the example of Wickes plc. This company was the victim of a fraud a few years ago. Indeed the trial of those alleged to be responsible is still running. At an early stage the new management and directors decided that they would not pursue civil claims for damages because, taking all the circumstances into account, they considered it was not in the company's interests to do so. Often, suing and letting things take their course through the courts is the easy option.

Whatever the objectives, the first task of the lawyer is to obtain information. What has happened? Who did what, when, where, why and how?

Information is not the same as evidence. How to obtain evidence is the subject of a separate paper, but the firm must always be alive to the need to collect evidence to support its client's case or damage the opponent's.

To this end steps need to be taken urgently at the beginning of an investigation into money laundering or fraud to preserve documents and all computer generated or stored material especially emails, audio tapes and video tapes. Any document-destruction policy must be suspended immediately. Bearing in mind, in an international case, the differences in time zones, co-ordination of such activity so that it happens simultaneously can be of vital importance to avoid tipping off accomplices and giving them time to destroy evidence.

Assets which may be the product of the crimes need to be identified and preserved – if necessary by going to courts in the relevant countries. Similar considerations of timing apply as to the preservation of evidence. Otherwise the risk is run that assets will be moved on and disappear.

These are areas where effective management and co-ordination of cross-border legal work is at a premium. Lawyers in different states need to work to a common plan, taking into account the different jurisdictional and procedural rules of their respective countries. They must be consistent in the actions they take and the pleas and arguments made.

In some countries a complaint to the local prosecutor can lead to the authorities taking swift action to restrict the movements of suspects and "freeze" their assets – much more quickly and cheaply than is the case in England, where this invariably requires an application to the court by the aggrieved person. Some years ago, I was involved in a case in which a bond dealer employed by a leading bank had committed a significant fraud. He fled to Switzerland where it was believed he had transferred his ill-gotten gains. A complaint to the Swiss police led to his arrest for questioning and the freezing of his Swiss bank account. All of this was done more quickly and effectively – and certainly more cheaply – than the clients and their UK and US lawyers could have managed unaided.

In some countries, court procedures at this stage are private, whilst in others they are public. Is publicity welcome or unimportant? Whichever the case, there may be options to be pursued elsewhere. Sometimes, it is an advantage to let the suspect know he is being chased. On other occasions the opposite is true, especially if more time is needed to build the case against him. One important consideration will be whether there is a continuing risk of further criminal activity.

5. LIAISON WITH AUTHORITIES

I have touched already on the possibility of enlisting the help of the authorities, but there is a need to spend a little more time on the question of liaison.

The first and most important question is whether there is a duty to make a report to the police or a regulator. In the UK, as part of the nation's response to the threat of money laundering, it is the duty of certain professionals to report suspicion of money laundering to the police. The class of people affected by this duty is to be extended following the second EU money laundering directive. This, however, is an exception to the rule. It is not generally the case that there is a duty to report crime to the police in the UK. Other countries have different rules and this needs to be considered in each case.

Even if there is no duty to report, is it advisable to do so? Can the authorities help?

I have already given the example of the help the Swiss police gave in a fraud case. One of the considerations is that they have a different set or priorities and interests. They may as much hinder as help.

What of others? A publicly listed company may have an obligation to make an announcement if what has happened if sufficiently material. Banks, bond holders, and other creditors may need to be informed too. In the case of an international business, that could be a formidable task and lawyers in a number of countries might have to be consulted as to the nature of any report and its content so that this is correct in local terms. There may be a need to reconcile what it is appropriate to report to third parties and what it is in the interests of the investigation and later prospects of achieving the company's objectives to reveal. Lawyers do not like to reveal their hand before they have to in case they give their opponents an advantage.

Finally, it will be necessary to see if there is any applicable insurance cover, for example, fidelity insurance. If there is, then before anything is done, insurers should be informed of what has happened so that their interests are not prejudiced and action may be co-ordinated with them.

In any case, there may be a question about the responsibility of third parties, for example, colleagues within the business who have not done what they should have done to protect the company's position and assets. The auditors may have been negligent. There may be insurance cover available to such third parties and, if so, there may be a need to give notice of a possible claim so that it is reported to insurers and they are thereby put on notice. This may be especially important if there is a risk of cover no longer remaining available when insurance markets are in turmoil, cover is increasingly hard to get and most policies apply on a claims-made basis.

6.   REPUTATION AND PR

We have seen only too graphically in the last 12 months what can happen to global corporations of apparent solidity and success when business crime is seen to have occurred within them. Nor is this phenomenon new. In Britain several years ago, Barings Bank was destroyed by a fraud. Personal reputations and livelihoods are broken too.

Not all businesses which are affected by fraud, corruption or money laundering are destroyed utterly, but they may still suffer grievous harm. Legal steps can only do so much to help and in any event the legal process is usually a long one. Other things may have to be done – new management brought in a visible demonstration to stamp out previous bad practices given, and press and PR management implemented.

There is often a need to co-ordinate the legal activities with what needs to be said publicly to explain to investors, suppliers and customers what has happened and what is being done. Neither line of activity should impede the other, and this requires close working together and exchange of information – within the limits of what is legally possible.

7. MULTI-JURISDICTIONAL ISSUES

As already stated, there are different ways of doing things in each country.
The first starting point is usually to decide in which court to bring the main case. There may well be other courts in other countries where interim measures will be sought to protect and preserve assets and evidence. Such matters are regulated in the European Union and the European Economic Area by a regulation and by the Brussels and Lugano Conventions. In respect of other countries there is no similar multinational solution, and it needs close work with lawyers in the local states to work out what is possible and advisable.

This needs to be done – and the whole inquiry managed – in the knowledge that there are different rules governing professional secrecy, or legal professional privilege, in each country. What may be withheld from disclosure in one country may not be in another. This is not only a difference between civil and common law approaches. There are significant variations between the US and UK on such issues.

These points are also clear in respect of disclosure of documents or discovery as it is often known. This is a process that is hardly known in civil law countries. In them, the notion that a party to litigation has to disclose documents which are adverse to his interest is greeted often with incredulity and dismay. In the US the scope of discovery is even wider that in England. It extends to the interrogation of witnesses on deposition and is regarded by many as extremely intrusive, burdensome and costly.

Finally, on this section, there is the need to observe the law in each place where information and evidence is being sought. This may appear an obvious point, but it is overlooked from time to time deliberately or by inadvertence.

A few years ago, the English High Court was presented with an issue about reports on a suspect's bank accounts obtained in breach of Swiss banking laws and the English Data Protection Act. The court was asked to order that the reports, which were in the hands of the plaintiffs' lawyers and privileged, be produced to the defendant, because they had been obtained as part of a criminal or fraudulent act. The court agreed. The law report does not disclose whether the court permitted reliance on the reports after that, but it illustrates the importance of behaving properly in each country or state concerned.

The law that is relevant in the UK for this purpose and the type of which is likely to be repeated in many countries includes: the Data Protection Act 1998, the Protection from Harassment Act 1997, the Computer Misuse Act 1990, the Regulation of Investigatory Powers Act, the Human Rights Act 1998, and the common law relating to breach of confidence, trespass, nuisance and copyright. Some countries have, unlike the UK, laws giving a right of privacy which will have a significant impact on the ability to garner information.

8.   CLIENTS' OBJECTIVES AND STRATEGY

I have already mentioned the need to establish objectives and strategy at an early stage. It is worth making the point that once fixed it should not be assumed that they remain good for ever. They should be re-evaluated when new information of importance comes to light and as the inquiry progresses. Directors and management have their own legal responsibilities and need to keep these in mind. In England they are said to have fiduciary duties, i.e. to act in the best interests of the company of which they are directors. Lawyers can help directors discharge those duties. Such help is particularly useful if a director is possibly subject to conflicting duties. In addition, and as one aspect of this, there will be occasions when a director occupies that function both in the holding company and also in a subsidiary which has been the victim of some form of business crime. That director must act in the best interests of the subsidiary, especially if there are other interests involved, e.g. banks. If he cannot satisfy the requirements of both companies, then he must resign. The company's lawyers can help him see what he must do, although clearly they cannot advise him personally.

9.   THE LAWYER'S DUTY

As in the discussion above about the director's position, it is to act in the best interest of the client and not to take advantage of the client or to put his own interest first. That means that however much he becomes interested and enthusiastic about the work on the case, he must remain objective and independent about the effect of the evidence, the prospects of success, the value of what is being done and achieved, weighed against the costs of getting thus far and likely to be incurred. If that means that he concludes that a particular line of inquiry is unsuccessful or likely to be so; or, that the objective sought by the client (for instance, a quick settlement) is unlikely to be achieved, then he must not hesitate to advise the client accordingly.

The lawyer must always act within the law and with propriety. This is so not only for his own sake, but because of the consequences for the client if he fails to do so.

Finally, the lawyer must not forget that he has his own legal responsibilities, not just professionally under his bar rules. I refer in particular to the duties under the money laundering rules in the United Kingdom, which may have now or shortly their equivalents in other countries. A British lawyer has an obligation to report suspicion of money laundering even if his client does not or does not wish him to. It is a criminal offence for him to fail to do so if he has reasonable grounds for suspecting that a money laundering offence has taken place. This is an objective standard, so that even if he did not form the suspicion, because he was negligent in not realising that he had grounds for so suspecting, he has still committed an offence. In the money laundering example I gave earlier, both lawyer and client would have had independent obligations to report their suspicions.

Care also needs to be taken over who is told that a report has been made. This is because there are legal prohibitions about "tipping off" a suspect. It is a criminal offence for someone to tell another that, for example, a report has been made about him to the National Criminal Intelligence Service. A lawyer cannot therefore do anything which may have the effect of warning a client that a report has been made about him. The safest course then for the lawyer is to act in accordance with the directions of NCIS – not the happiest basis for a lawyer-client relationship, but regarded by Parliament as a necessary consequence of the fright against crime and terrorism.

3

Transnational commercial bribery:
Challenge to arbitration

By Mark Pieth
Professor of Criminal Law and Criminology,
University of Basel, Switzerland;
Chairman of the OECD Working Group
on Combating Corruption

1.   CORRUPTION AND ARBITRATION

With a good sense for timing, the ICC Institute of World Business Law has chosen the topic "Arbitration – Money Laundering, Corruption and Fraud" for its Annual Meeting 2002. In particular, the issue of corruption has been a difficult one for arbitrators to deal with in the past, in a world of endemic bribery and double standards. Traditionally, arbitrators have placed great emphasis on the principle of the autonomy of parties and have in general honoured contracts, even where substantial indicators have pointed towards bribery. This may be understandable under the circumstances: extortionate conditions exist in many developing and emerging economies, and there is widespread tolerance of foreign bribery by countries of the North.

For approximately the last decade, however, international policy has been changing dramatically. A plethora of initiatives has been taken to outlaw bribery. This raises the question of where that leaves arbitrators who are, for instance, expected by the parties to legitimate inflated commissions to intermediaries or to condone only lightly camouflaged bribery arrangements. To the international community and countries which have adopted new anti-corruption policies, the answer matters a great deal, since many of the most significant business contracts – and some of the most delicate deals (such as defence or large-scale construction contracts) – are subject to arbitration agreements.

This text gives an overview of the changing international standards and their domestic implementation from the perspective of international policy, in order to raise the question of how arbitrators are affected by such changes.

2. A DECADE OF INITIATIVES

Whereas earlier initiatives against bribery failed dramatically[1], the opening of Eastern Europe and the quickening pace of globalisation have apparently created the momentum needed to do away with those undemocratic leaders who were previously pampered for geopolitical reasons, but are now suddenly perceived as irrational impediments to trade by many exporters and investors. This shift of attitude opened the way for both international financial institutions (IFI) and inter-governmental organisations, helped along by non-governmental organisations and representatives of the private sector, to develop anti-corruption policies.

Shortly after 1990, first the World Bank and then the regional development banks adopted general anti-corruption policies, as well as specific rules, particularly in the area of IFI-funded procurement. To many people, these policy initiatives came as a surprise, since IFIs had a long-standing reputation of turning a blind eye to corrupt practices. It must be pointed out, however, that the World Bank developed one of the strictest and most feared anti-corruption tools by threatening to exclude companies caught bribing using contracts funded by the World Bank[2]. Recent cases in Southern Africa have underscored that not just small and medium sized enterprises, but also multinational enterprises, are vulnerable and that their legal and reputational risk has been increased significantly by the new policies.

Also, during the last decade of the 20th century, a multitude of action plans, declarations, recommendations and conventions against corruption have been adopted. Depending on the specific mandate of the international organisations, their scope and their methodology, these initiatives have diverging rationales. So far, very little thought has gone into the idea of developing an "integrated architecture" of international standards against corruption. A series of regional initiatives, especially in Europe and the Americas, has generated far-reaching policies, covering domestic and foreign, active and passive, public and private corruption as well as related behaviour such as trafficking in influence.

This comprehensive approach, primarily developed in the criminal law conventions of the OAS[3] and of the Council of Europe[4], above all attempts to harmonise standards regionally in order to facilitate mutual legal assistance and extradition.

The goal of the various EU conventions against corruption[5], on the other hand, is far more restricted, aiming to safeguard the financial interests of the Union against all sorts of tax evasion and subsidy manipulation.

More recently, the UN has initiated a new attempt to develop a worldwide convention. Even though the drafts cover a multitude of issues, the Convention will hardly go beyond a worldwide minimum standard and it remains unclear whether a credible follow-up mechanism can be devised. Its actual contribution, beyond that of extending the coverage of regional conventions, will be the development of procedures for the repatriation of embezzled and defrauded funds from financial centres to the victim states.

The OECD Revised Recommendation of 1997, as well as the Convention of 1997[6], touches upon the responsibility of both natural and legal persons, and contemplates a wide variety of sanctions, including the confiscation of bribes and the profits from bribery. Furthermore, it criminalizes accounting offences and bribery-related money laundering.

3.   OUTLAWING CORRUPTION IN INTERNATIONAL COMMERCE

The common denominator of all these efforts is to raise the stakes for both corruptors and recipients by outlawing their practices. Therefore, much depends on the ability of international policy *fora* to transform the legal landscape in a relatively short time and to make the threat credible by ensuring the application of national anti-corruption laws.

Within international organisations, this goal is primarily approached by "peer evaluation" of national performance. Monitoring is the key word for the OECD[7], the Council of Europe[8] and, more recently, also, the OAS. The most advanced form of monitoring currently available is probably the "OECD Phase II" –monitoring[9], based on a lengthy, written, preparatory procedure (self-evaluation through questionnaires), an on-site visit, with interviews conducted by two countries nominated as "lead examiners" in conjunction with secretariat experts and, finally, a hearing in the OECD Working Group on Bribery, where the ultimate formulation of the report is decided.

Recent struggles to secure the necessary funding for this meaningful, but expensive, process have clearly demonstrated that the need for strict monitoring is not easily understood by all the Member Governments. It is largely due to pressure by the private sector and non-governmental pressure groups (especially the NGO Transparency International) that the budget necessary for Phase II evaluations could be secured at all.

Of course, it would be too simplistic to expect that a worldwide change of attitude could be brought about simply by encouraging law enforcement agencies to start investigations on the behaviour of exporters and investors abroad. The approaches of the OECD and of regional conventions, to the extent they focus on commercial bribery, primarily seek to foster change within companies and their trading practices.

Some very difficult questions need to be addressed by the private sector. Whereas the issue of where to draw the line between bribery and gifts, entertainment, etc. may appear to be a comparatively easy task, defining policies for political and social payments may cause more difficulty. Furthermore, it is vital that companies develop concepts to prevent bribery through third parties, especially foreign subsidiaries, agents or joint venture partners. They will have to define, for such intermediaries, the selection criteria, the terms of contract, the manner of reviewing such contracts, the ways of remunerating agent services, etc. In brief, experts and investors are faced with the difficult task of defining internal compliance concepts and transmitting the message to all branches and all employees of the company, worldwide.

4.   INDUSTRY STANDARDS: GOING BEYOND THE SINGLE HOUSE

It has become increasingly evident that even large companies risk the loss of entire markets if they attempt to "go it alone." They may easily be outflanked by less scrupulous competitors. Therefore, the idea of developing so-called "industry standards" is becoming increasingly popular. Whereas ICC and NGOs have been working on neutral blueprints and abstract standards[10], some sectors have been experimenting with setting more concrete standards. The model first emerged in the financial services industry on a different, if related, topic: the prevention of the abuse of private banking for money laundering purposes, leading to the formulation of the Wolfsberg Principles[11]. Ongoing efforts in other areas, especially civil engineering, power systems, defence and energy, are drawing from these experiences. The methodology used is, in theory, relatively simple: outside facilitators encourage executives of key players in a given sector to exchange information on their anti-corruption compliance and to identify the particularly problematic issues in their specific field of activity. They encourage the companies to develop a mutual understanding on best practices, especially in relation to the issues of third parties and fringe issues like political and social payments. Once the companies have agreed on such best practices, the pressure amongst members of the "club" to conform is usually such that more formal monitoring of compliance is not necessary. In areas with smaller units, for instance the engineering professions, alternative avenues have been explored, especially the option of having compliance certified by outside experts[12].

Industry standards are a necessary complement to international public standards, laws and regulations. Together they offer a real chance of large-scale change in the foreseeable future.

5.   HOW DOES CHANGE AFFECT ARBITRATORS?

It may be concluded that even though corruption is still widespread in many regions of the world, an internationally agreed *ordre public* banning bribery is emerging.

Arbitrators confronted with indicia of bribery are faced with a series of difficult decisions: they are forced to evaluate their own jurisdiction. One way of dealing with corruption would be to refuse jurisdiction to arbitrate and to refer the issue back to the public courts. Other questions will arise, of course, if they do accept jurisdiction, relating to the standards of evidence on bribery. If the arbitration panel does pronounce itself, it will have to deal with the question of whether international public standards will have pre-eminence over any law of the parties' choice. If such pre-eminence is recognised, the precise legal consequences remain to be determined. Nullity of the meta-contract, the bribe contract, may allow the nullification of the underlying contract, but this result is hardly likely to be accorded automatic effect, since the victim may well prefer to save the contract[13].

Apart from such considerations, arbitrators have to examine with great care if they – for example, by adjudicating a highly suspicious commission – could become accessories to the corrupt dealings. This eventuality, in particular, needs to be examined closely where the territorially applicable public law bans corrupt gratuities (payments as consideration for acting or omitting to act in the exercise of the official's duty)[14]. In such a case, a judge or an arbitrator intentionally ordering a party to honour a bribe contract may risk criminal prosecution.

FOOTNOTES

1   Cf. UN 1975-79 (Ecosoc).

2   See para. 1.15 of the World Bank's procurement guidelines.

3   Inter-American Convention Against Corruption of 29/3/1996.

4   Criminal Law Convention on Corruption (ETS No. 173, 27/1/199); Civil Law Convention on Corruption (ETS No. 174, 4/11/1999).

5   Convention on the Protection of the European Community's Financial Interests (C 316, 27/11/1995, 9.49 ff.); Protocol I (C 313, 23/10/1996); Protocol II (C 212, 19/7/1997); Convention on the Fight Against Corruption Involving Officials of the European Communities or Officials of Member States of the European Union (C197 25/6/1997).

6   Revised Recommendation of the Council on Bribery in International Business Transactions, 23/5/1994; Convention on Combating Bribery of Foreign Public Officials in International Business Transactions, 21/11/1997.

7   Recommendation VIII; Convention Art. 12.

8   With its GRECO instrument.

9   Aiolfi/Pieth, "How To Make a Convention Work: The OECD Recommendation and Convention on Bribery as an Example of a New Horizon in International Law," in: Fijnaut/Huberts, *Corruption, Integrity and Law Enforcement*, The Hague 2002, p. 249 ff.

10 See Transparency International and Social Accountability International, Business Principles for Countering Bribery, December 2002.

11 Pieth/Aiolfi, "The Private Sector Become Active: The Wolfsberg Process," in *A Practitioner's Guide to International Money Laundering, Law and Regulation*, London 2003.

12 Take the example of FIDIC.

13 For a detailed discussion of these issues, see. Abdulay Sayed, *Corruption in International Trade and Commercial Arbitration*, Geneva 2001.

14 Cf. for instance Art. 322[septies], Swiss Criminal Code.

4

The 1997 OECD Convention against transnational bribery:
Effective monitoring and implementation

By Giorgio Sacerdoti
Professor of International Law, Bocconi University, Milan, Italy;
Former Vice President, OECD Working Group
on Combating Corruption;
Member of the Appellate Board of the WTO

1. THE ROLE OF THE OECD IN COMBATING CORRUPTION IN INTERNATIONAL BUSINESS IN THE GLOBAL ECONOMY

The OECD Convention on 'Combating bribery of foreign public officials in international business transactions' signed in Paris on 17 December 1997 (in force since 15 February 1999) represents a major tangible result of a series of international initiatives developed as a number of scandals and investigations revealed, under pressure from global public opinion, the problem of corruption in international affairs.

The OECD Convention covers a narrower range of offences than other conventions, such a the one of the Council of Europe (1999) or that between the Members of the European Union (1997), neither of which is yet in force, since it criminalizes only active corruption besides punishing related offences (money laundering and false accounting). On the other hand, it is in force in all the Members of the OECD plus five other countries, 34 countries in total, and it covers corruption of public officials of any State, not just of the States parties on the basis of reciprocity as is the case for the EU Convention.

As is well known, the work of the OECD in this area began in 1989 at the initiative of the US, whose companies were concerned by the fact that they were the only ones subject to criminal sanctions for bribes paid abroad under the 'Foreign

Corrupt Practices Act' (FCPA) of 1977. In almost all other countries, the offence of corruption was aimed only at safeguarding the integrity of the local public administration. Criminalizing the corruption of foreign officials was not provided for, even where the conduct would involve international transactions and the economic interest of several countries. This is the case where, thanks to corruption, a company obtains a market abroad to the detriment of more deserving competitors of a third country. It is not only commercial arguments which justify the international expansion of the sphere of action of the rules against corruption. Other relevant factors are the growing interdependence of economies, financial co-operation in favour of developing countries with use of public funds, the emergence of common values of good government, transparency of public administration, and democracy. In this context, the lack of interest displayed until recently by a number of the largest countries which dispose of effective intervention instruments on the supply side, i.e. as regards their companies which export to and invest abroad, was difficult to justify further.

In the global economy this "benign neglect" cannot be justified with the contention that it is principally up to each State to "assure that its own house is in order", and that practices and sensibilities are not the same everywhere with regard to a phenomenon which is narrowly linked to the political and adminis-trative organization of each country.

International co-operation is necessary in order to cope effectively with these negative side effects of globalisation. Successful operation of such a convention in the hands of like-minded States and their enforcing authorities means that global business can be policed effectively, by addressing the white-collar crimi-nality which may be associated with (and facilitated by) the opening up of economies and the easiness and lack of controls surrounding most transnational trade and financial transactions. On the other hand, unilateral actions by a single country incriminating behaviours outside of its territory (even if enforcement only intervenes within) is open to criticism of interference, and all the more so when high political figures of a foreign country (such as the head of State or ministers) are called into question. Unilateral action can also reveal itself to be ineffective in practice when the proceeding country (such as the US under the FCPA) institutes criminal sanctions against corruption abroad in isolation. The legal and factual limitations (for example as regards the collection of evidence) of the (even indirect) extra-territorial exercise of the national penal jurisdiction are well known, especially where the authorities of other countries involved do not collaborate. Business and investment freedom, the use of groups and companies with subsidiaries in offshore centres and the recourse to obliging intermediaries permit companies to elude obligations enacted in the country where they have their head office when international co-operation is lacking. In any case, while unilateralism may be successful in the case of the United States, thanks to its economic and political position of a world power, this is not so for the majority of other countries.

The aim was therefore at OECD that of organizing effective co-operation between the principal actors in the international economy to promulgate an effective legal instrument containing reciprocal and comparable legal commitments to combat transnational bribery, building a consensus based on shared objectives[1].

2. NEGOTIATION AND ENTRY IN FORCE OF THE CONVENTION

An *ad hoc* Working Group was established for this purpose by the OECD in 1989. It was successful after many years of preparatory work to draft the text of a treaty (1997), supported by the political will of the Member States[2]. The Working Group is still the focal point of OECD activities in the field, especially as to the monitoring of compliance by the member countries of their commit-ment to implement effectively the Convention and the related indications of the 1994 Recommendation, revised in 1997.

The finalization of the Convention's text in 1996-97, its signature on 17 December of the same year and its entering into force in early 1999, followed by ratification of all signatories within 2001, was a remarkable achievement. It is enough to think of the initial political perplexities voiced in many countries and of the difficult legal problems, due to different traditions (such as on jurisdiction and on the liability of companies) that had to be overcome. The negotiators managed to resolve these difficulties also by drafting explanatory notes, later transformed to become "Commentaries" on the Convention, and adopted at the same time as the text of the Convention by the Negotiation Conference[3]. However, these Commentaries do not form part of the Convention and have not been signed. Furthermore, they do not have an organic character as do, for example, the explanatory Reports of the conventions of the Council of Europe, and only refer to certain articles of the OECD Conven-tion or to individual clauses.

The weight which should be granted to these "Commentaries" in interpreting the Convention has been discussed. In our opinion, they are not "preparatory documents" to which one can have recourse as a supplementary interpretation tool pursuant to Article 32 of the Vienna Convention on the Law of Treaties of 1969, which codified traditional international law in this area. They are rather, and more significantly, a basic element of the "context" within which the OECD Convention was drafted for the purpose of interpretation pursuant to Article 31 of the Vienna Convention. As for the context, Article 31 mentions any agree-ment relating to a treaty which is entered into by all the parties in connection with the conclusion of such treaty. I doubt whether the Commentaries can be considered to be really an agreement "in simplified form", for the simple reason that it was the specific intention of the contracting parties not to insert the content of the Commentaries in the Convention. However, the "context" is not limited to such an agreement relating to a treaty but includes also other instruments. The Commentaries thus provide guidance in determining, in the event of doubt, the scope of the Convention, although they would not constitute an authentic interpretation. The Commentaries have been in fact relied on by various countries in drafting implementing legislation for the Convention.

3. GENERAL FEATURES OF THE CONVENTION

The Convention is principally characterized (and this is a novelty) by the fact that the industrialized countries in which most large multinational companies are based have bound themselves to prevent and repress bribery by their companies, by criminalizing "active" corruption (that is, bribing) in respect of other countries officials (whether signatory or not), independently of the applicability and enforcement of criminal laws in the latter countries to the "passive" corruption of those officials (that is, taking a bribe). The contracting States thereby do not intend to admit the corruption of these foreign officials, nor any tolerance of such behaviour by the States to which they belong. They just took note of the fact that pursuing the officials themselves would have raised insoluble jurisdictional issues and would have opened them up to the criticism of interfering with the sovereignty of other States[4].

This approach is also based on economic and trade concerns, that is, avoiding that international competition be distorted by the recourse to measures considered to be inadmissible. According to a popular expression, the objective is to guarantee the "levelling of the playing field", i.e. to assure common playing rules for companies of different origins in international markets in this regard. The harmonisation of criminal rules, especially when the initiative originates from a group of leading countries rather than from the action of a multilateral institution, is not common. It demonstrates a new orientation in the multi-lateral regulation of international trade in general, even if there have been precedents such as, for example, the fight against money laundering. The OECD Convention, open for adhesion to other countries as indicated by Article 13 (2), represents a model for further initiatives, notably the worldwide convention against corruption which is being currently negotiated at the UN.

Before the principal provisions of the text are discussed, another general characteristic of the Convention must be noted. It closely follows the model of the classic penal law conventions (such as those of the Council of Europe or against terrorism) in defining the offence, the jurisdictional basis, the secondary rules and the organization of mutual co-operation between member States in matters of assistance and extradition. However, the OECD Convention distances itself from the traditional model in different respects. First, its norms are not self-executing. In particular, the rule providing for the criminalization of the corruption of foreign public officials, provided by Article 1, has generally required reformulation in order to be introduced in the criminal legislation of the member States. Similarly, other rules regarding the extent and type of sanctions, jurisdiction and statutes of limitation are not formulated exhaustively, but indicate the fundamental content, which the national implementing rules will have to respect.

This approach is not fortuitous. The negotiators had to take note of the fact that the criminal systems of different States were inspired by different criteria on a number of crucial matters, such as the subjection of legal persons to criminal law, the extension of jurisdictional competence on the basis of the nationality of the person charged or, on the contrary, solely on a territorial basis, and the obligatory or discretionary character of criminal prosecution. Given the method followed in the Convention, stated in the preamble, of combating the evil of corruption through equivalent national measures, the member States can fulfil their obligations by having recourse to different measures depending on their legislative structure, on the condition that these are adequate to attain the prescribed result[5].

Secondly, the Convention also contains non-criminal rules, more specifically as to the requirements for corporate accounting and auditing, with a transparency and preventive purpose. Finally, the convention provides for a multilateral supervisory role for the OECD Group on corruption, to promote and monitor the full implementation of the Convention through the periodic examinations of measures adopted and their concrete application by States. This mechanism replaces a procedure for the settlement of disputes, often present in criminal conventions. It appears more flexible and efficient to ensure the respect of reciprocal commitments and, in general, the realization of the Convention's objectives. It aims, and this point must be emphasized, not just at introducing criminal rules in the legislation of signatories countries, but more specifically at deterring, preventing and combating international corruption, an element of serious global concern, through effective national co-ordinated measures.

4. THE OFFENCE OF ACTIVE BRIBERY OF FOREIGN PUBLIC OFFICIALS

The Convention contains, in Article 1, the obligation to establish the corruption of foreign public officials as an offence in the same manner as the corruption of national officials is criminalized in domestic law. The Convention includes preventive and repressive accompanying rules, which may require the update of provisions relating to internal corruption as well. In conformity with the non-self-executing approach of the Convention, the Commentaries specify that the undertaking can be implemented through different means, such as on the basis of a law which would punish corruption in general, or by extending the application of the offence of corruption of national public agents in the penal code, or by having recourse to *ad hoc* provisions, as in the case of the US with the FCPA.

Article 1 (1) of the text defines the offence as "the act of offering, promising or giving an undue advantage, whether pecuniary or not, to a foreign public official, for that official or for a third party, in order for him to act or to refrain from acting in relation to the performance of official duties, in order to obtain or retain business or other improper advantage in the conduct of international business"[6].

Thus a bribe can consist of a gift besides an amount of money; it is irrelevant moreover whether it is given to a third party (such as a relative, an institution or a political party), provided it is the *quid pro quo* of the improper conduct of the public official.

On the basis of Article 1 (2), complicity (participation) and incitement to corruption, including "authorization", also constitute criminal offences. For example, an authorization given by a parent company to a foreign subsidiary to pay a bribe will lead to the exercise of jurisdictional competence and application of criminal law against the former and/or any of its managers who are responsible.

A foreign public official is defined in Article 1 (3) as any person who – in a foreign country – holds a legislative, administrative or judicial office, or who exercises a public function for a foreign country, including a public agency or enterprise, and any official of an international organization. This is a wide definition, which combines subjective qualifications with the objective exercise of public functions in a manner similar to the approach taken by numerous national criminal legal systems. For example, this definition aims at taking into account the fact that the framework within which economic functions are directly exercised by the State varies from one country to another, and that, given the current progression of privatisation, the private sector is being entrusted functions which, objectively, are of a public nature.

The extension of the offence in respect of the behaviour of managers of companies, which are private but controlled by the State, gave rise to discussions and it was not possible to insert supplemental specifications in the text. The commentary specifies that a company is deemed "public" if it is one on which the State can exercise a dominant influence, something which can be done by different means. In addition, it is specified that the person responsible in such a company does exercise a public function, unless the company operates as a private company on a normal commercial basis and without State support.

The offence must be punished by each State by "effective, proportionate and dissuasive criminal penalties", including imprisonment, which are to be equivalent to those provided for the corruption of national public officials. The application of other punitive measures, such as seizure and confiscation of the bribe and of the proceeds of the bribery, is to be provided for[7].

5.   THE RESPONSIBILITY OF COMPANIES

With reference to the author of the offence, the text of the Convention in Articles 2 and 3 addresses the central question of the responsibility of companies which bribe, or for whose benefit such payment are made, in light of the fact that the criminal responsibility of a company is recognized only by certain legal systems.

The Convention does not impose an obligation to introduce criminal responsibility of legal persons in countries where it is not recognized, an obligation that
would have exceeded its scope. States which do not recognize the criminal
responsibility of companies have committed themselves to introduce effective,
proportionate and dissuasive non-criminal (essentially pecuniary) sanctions. This
should limit the risk of divergence between countries where companies are
subject to criminal law and countries where they are not. Just introducing non-
criminal sanctions applicable to companies where such a system does not exist in
general entails substantive legislative changes, as the experience of some
signatories in complying (notably Italy) has shown. The question of jurisdictional
competence in this non-criminal administrative matter also arises, and finally that
of the level of the penalties. As regards this last aspect, non-pecuniary sanctions
such as the exclusion from participation in invitations to tender, or the deprivation
of directors of their functions when they are guilty even just for lack of due
diligence, could be more effective than criminal sanctions applied only to the
managers responsible[8].

6.   JURISDICTIONAL CRITERIA

The other delicate point is that of the criteria for determining jurisdiction, which
was debated at great length throughout the negotiation, with a view to achieving
a balance between the obligations of the different signatory States, as well as a
balanced and effective enforcement. A number of predominantly civil law
countries such as France, Germany and Italy consider the nationality of the
defendant to be a criterion in determining jurisdiction so that they can prosecute
offences committed by their nationals abroad (given certain conditions). The US
has changed its traditional exercise of criminal jurisdiction on a purely territorial
basis, amending the FCPA so as to take into account nationality in order to
implement more fully the Convention.

Article 4 of the Convention requires States to prosecute the offence by applying
the legal criteria traditional to their own system. A balance in the way corrup-tion
is punished between countries with different legal systems should be obtained
through non-criminal penalties on companies, which may be imposed also in
case of strict territorial criminal jurisdiction, in all cases where bribe payment is
attributable to a company. The fact that these bribes have been promised or paid

abroad through an intermediary, or through subsidiaries which are not under the management of nationals of the home country, would not avoid prosecution in this respect.

7.   APPLICATION OF ANTI-MONEY LAUNDERING LEGISLATION

The reference to money laundering legislation in Article 7 of the Convention is crucial to its successful enforcement as well as for the prevention of bribery by making the hiding of the bribe and of the proceeds more risky and difficult.

Money laundering consists in the transferring of funds, gained in criminal activities or meant to commit crime, through international financial channels (banks and other intermediaries) hiding their origin through various passages with the complicity of institutions, trustees, professionals, etc.

Anti-laundering legislation was developed first against drug trafficking; it has been progressively extended to the transfer of proceeds of other serious crimes, as agreed internationally both under the auspices of a G7 Task Force operating within the OECD (FATF) and within the UN, from the late 1980's on. Measures agreed by all main industrialized countries, to which a few other States have adhered, include not only criminal law sanctions and mutual co-operation. They entail, crucially, the obligation of banks and similar institutions not to carry out suspicious deals (such as large cash transactions) and to report them secretly to police and prosecutors.

Where domestic corruption is a basis for the application of the money laundering legislation (which is currently the case in several countries and which is becoming the rule in several other States), Article 7 of the Convention requires the application of the same rules against the money laundering of funds to corruption of foreign public officials: it prescribes thus "national treatment" in this respect. This is a point which is fundamental to the effective application of the Convention. It is well known that bribery paid to high-ranking foreign officials are made "from abroad to abroad" by using banking channels and financial intermediaries in third countries, usually offshore financial centres protected by bank secrecy and hostile to international collaboration. These payments did not entail money laundering in the past, since transnational corruption was not a crime. Things have now changed. With the adherence to the OECD Convention of countries like Luxembourg and Switzerland (but not other non-co-operative offshore centres!), the local regulation against money laundering, including reporting and disclosure obligations as to a transaction, and seizure and confiscation of the funds, has become applicable when the offence of corruption of a foreign public official is at issue. Participating to such dubious financial transactions entails the risk of criminal responsibility.

The Commentary to the Convention explains that reference is made to the bribe both before the payment is made (i.e. funds earmarked for the illicit payment) and after they have been transferred and made available to the corrupt beneficiary. This is a significant specification. As the Convention only incriminates active corruption (that is, promising or giving a bribe), it was important to specify that the transfer of funds by the beneficiary after they are obtained (typically from the official to a bank) does not exempt this transaction from the rules against money laundering, as the money nevertheless remains the result of the offence of active corruption of a foreign public official.

8. ACCOUNTING AND FINANCIAL STATEMENTS OF COMPANIES

The provision of Article 8, which deals with companies' accounting, assumes a fundamental importance. It has a great practical and certainly innovative dimension, which goes beyond the penal framework and assumes a pre-dominantly preventive role. This Article prescribes that, in order to combat international corruption effectively:

1. "Each Party shall take such measures as may be necessary, within the framework of its laws and regulations regarding the maintenance of books and records, financial statement disclosures, and accounting and auditing standards, to prohibit the establishment of off-the-books or inadequately identified transactions, the recording of non-existent expenditures, the entry of liabilities with incorrect identi-fication of their object, as well as the use of false documents, by companies subject to those laws and regulations, for the purpose of bribing foreign public officials or of hiding such bribery.

2. Each Party shall provide effective, proportionate and dissuasive civil, administrative or criminal penalties for such omissions and falsifications in respect of the books, records, accounts, and financial statements of such companies."

The obligations in question are already found in national legislation in this area, as well as in the accounting principles applicable to large companies or listed corporations. However, there are practical difficulties in detecting suspect payments in a company's records and accounts.

The Group had made enquiries and commissioned studies between 1994 and 1997 as to this subject matter in order to grasp fully the issue. In fact, national legislation and practices which require large companies and in any case those listed in a stock exchange to maintain accounting books and financial records require that entries and other records be complete, accurate, detailed and systematic, listing correctly all payments made and received as well as their nature also in relation to international transactions, including payments to agents and other intermediaries. Those records are generally subject to internal and external audit: sanctions, in some cases even criminal sanctions, are imposed for record keeping violations.

However when irregularities are carried out it may be quite difficult to find them. Illegal payments will normally be disguised, often as commercial commissions or fees. Auditors do not look at every transaction. They generally check whether adequate procedures and internal controls are in place and applied. Moreover, auditors organize their work in order to discover errors, omissions and irregularities that are substantial enough to have a "material" impact on the financial statements, that is, which affect generally the financial statements. Not all incorrect payments, even of a large amount, will be discovered under this approach. Finally auditors usually do not have to disclose the results of their investigation to public authorities, except in regulated industries such as banking and insurance. The duty of confidentiality may even prevent auditors from doing so. Irregularities detected may have to be disclosed only to the management (which may be responsible for them), or to some committee of the board.

The purpose of Article 8 is in any case to reinforce the preventive function of the accounting requirement and of controls thereon in order to avoid that large sums of money be diverted from company accounts and used for "grand" corruption abroad, as has appeared from certain investigations in various countries in recent years.

Moreover, this provision should result in a re-examination by competent national authorities of the effectiveness of the controls (internal and upon audit) in place on accounting. The provision is also relevant, as the Commentary recalls, as to the consideration of potential liabilities in financial statements, and as to the discharge of their duties by auditors. In other words, after the entry into force of the Convention auditors would be liable if they have not detected corruption by properly examining a company's books and records.

The proper implementation of these obligations does not concern only non-criminal pecuniary sanctions as regards accounting, balance sheets and the auditing standards which apply (a matter which, in the European Union is included mostly within the competence of the Commission). Article 8.2 requires indeed the application of criminal sanctions for grave omissions, such as forgery, falsification and fraud.

9.   MUTUAL ASSISTANCE AND EXTRADITION

Effective mutual assistance is fundamental given the frequent use of inter-national financial channels to effect and hide transnational bribery. Article 9 on international judicial mutual assistance lays down an obligation for signatory States to reciprocally provide prompt and effective legal assistance, also as to non-criminal procedures. It requires them to keep the requesting authorities informed of the implementation of any request for judicial assistance (such as searches, transmission of documents, deposition by witnesses). This binding commitment will certainly be precious to the prosecutors and judges of foreign countries investigating or judging such cases. They are often disappointed by the lack of collaboration by other States and by the delays with which they get the information and documents sought. Provisions on co-operation are completed by the usual rules on extradition, which include an obligation for countries which refuse to extradite their nationals to prosecute them directly (Article 10 (3))[9].

10.   THE BUSINESS WORLD AND THE OECD CONVENTION

From the point of view of business, having recourse to bribery of officials of foreign countries in order to obtain international contracts and procurements has become a dangerous activity in OECD countries and by their enterprises, one to refrain from if the risk of prosecution and incrimination is to be avoided. The direct peril of criminal incrimination is not the only factor to take into account when evaluating the impact of the Convention on the conduct of international business. There are both side-aspects of criminal law to take into account, as well as the spill-off on the competitive climate. From the first point of view, the "successful" carrying out of transnational bribery implies relying on a network of intermediaries, such as agents, lawyers, fiduciaries and banks, in order to divert funds from corporate accounts, set up offshore companies, transfer the bribe and the proceeds through national borders hiding their illegal origin. With the new legal conventional framework in place in major countries, professionals should be wary of supplying their services for operations that pertain now to white-collar criminality. Serious banks should deny their financial channels for the purpose of carrying out transfers: money laundering reporting obligations should not be taken lightly by serious financial operators. Effective international co-operation under the Convention and under anti-money laundering instruments is now available to make illegal operations involving bribery highly risky and visible. In fact, recent scandals involving Russian and Indonesian (to name only some) banks, companies and politicians show that secrecy in this respect is becoming more difficult.

Also from the point of view of international competition, the Convention may or should become a relevant instrument. Up to now a company that had reasons to believe that it had lost a foreign deal due to corruption by a competitor had no direct action for redress, especially if it had no full evidence, as is normally the case. This may now change if the Convention is properly implemented and its provisions are taken seriously by companies operating in world market. Options now open are the following:

- to make a denunciation in the country of the public official (this was possible before, but may be ineffective or even risky);

- to make a denunciation with the competent public prosecutor of the country of the head office of the corrupt competitor in order that an investigation be opened, since the bribing is a crime there;

- to make a claim for damages in a civil court against the competitor in its home country as a consequence of the illegal action of bribery.

On the other hand, the action of bribery by a manager is now unlawful, and detecting action and compliance programs are necessary in order to avoid corporate responsibility towards investigating authorities; loss of benefits and contracts as sanction; actions against incompetent auditors for failure to discover and evidence incorrect accounting, false statements and illegal payments; and *dulcis in fundo* derivative suits by shareholders.

Taking such an action is unpopular in business circles, as is well known; equivalent actions may be envisaged. Leaking to the press the facts would entail an obligation of prosecutors in the home country to act in most cases, although examples of these initiatives are still lacking. Actions by authorities in home countries may give courage to prosecutors in the country of the public official to enforce more effectively their laws against local corrupt politicians.

11. MONITORING AND IMPLEMENTING THE CONVENTION

The effectiveness of any legal and enforcement action as to transnational bribery has often aroused perplexity (to say the least), as economic crime takes on a global scale whereas States tend to act in a dispersed manner. When assessing the effectiveness of the Convention, one can not therefore ignore the creation of a mechanism of constant monitoring and follow-up entrusted by Article 12 on the OECD Working Group on corruption in international business.

The monitoring process at OECD is meant to ensure that the equivalent obligations undertaken by the participants to the Convention be carried out fully and evenly thanks to their domestic enforcing legislation and prosecution activity. This monitoring activity falls within the wide range of "national compliance monitoring and reporting" activity that many international organ-izations carry out as to treaty and other obligations in many areas. The moni-toring of compliance of human rights obligations by UN bodies is the most prominent, but many other examples are available. The legal obligations involved in these mechanisms vary, as is the case for the legal consequences of non- compliance, the format and effect of the reports issued and the level of openness to the public. In all cases, one may venture to say that the "reputation" effects, the echo in the public opinion and through the press, and the reaction of NGOs may be more important to induce compliance than formal legal considerations.

The OECD model does reflect these experiences. The Working Group relies on a combination of detailed technical assessment by the Secretariat, of confidential "peer pressure" by fellow members and finally of public disclosure of the Group's evaluation and reporting of each country's compliance. Through a procedure of mutual review of national implementation measures and application practice, the Working Group systematically monitors the respect for the obligations subscribed to by the contracting States, and the effectiveness of the application of the Convention by each of them in actually combating transnational bribery. This is an important mutual assurance that the solemn commitment subscribed to by all industrialized OECD countries to render their territories "off-limits" to such practices shall be carried out.

Has the Working Group been successful? How do you measure success in this respect? What about the recent criticism voiced by representatives of some countries, that not all countries do enforce seriously the Convention? What about the view expressed by Transparency International that the business world (notably major multinational companies) based in the OECD countries are not taking the Convention obligations seriously? That transnational bribery flourishes, that small and medium enterprises often ignore its very existence?

As to the tasks of the Working Group, I will recall that it has already completed "Phase 1" of the monitoring process: the review of participants implementing legislation was carried out between 1999 and 2002 and was duly reported through the OECD "Committee on International Investment and Multinational Enterprises" (CIME) to the OECD governing body, the Ministerial Council, in 2000, 2001 and 2002[10]. These examinations have been a serious exercise, putting strain on the examined countries: each time detailed reports on all relevant point of implementing legislation, in respect of each Convention provisions, have been prepared by the Secretariat based on the lengthy answers to specific questionnaires by each country. The answers have been checked with relevant legislation, two countries in turn have been appointed for each examined country with the task of checking the most delicate issues and leading the discussion, as "lead examiners", within the Group at meetings devoted to these examinations, country after country. Political considerations of "comity" have played no role.

Each final report contains an "evaluation" of the implementing legislation, which points to specific issues where, as often has been the case, the Group has detected shortcomings, to the need for correction or completion or expressing doubts which should be dispelled through appropriate application in the future.
The final reports with the evaluations have been made public and have been

the basis for open criticism and pressure by other governments, through the press and by public opinion, to seek and obtain completion and changes of domestic legislation when found inadequate by the Group. The cases of the United Kingdom and of Japan may be singled out in this respect as examples of subsequent adoption of further legislation by some members in view of the shortcomings detected by the Group and the criticisms voiced at those countries[11].

The subsequent stage of monitoring by the Working Group is the so called Phase 2. It involves a detailed review of implementation practice, notably by means of encounters with the national judicial and administrative authorities entrusted with enforcement, thus making multilateral monitoring fully effective. As of mid-2002, Phase 2 monitoring had been carried out for Finland and the US, and was proceeding for Germany.

Finally, an important result of Phase 1 monitoring are the conclusions that the Group has drawn as to possible shortcomings of the Convention itself in the light of an "horizontal" comparison of the review of the various national implementing legislations. The Group has reflected on this issue especially with a view to the aim of the Convention to ensure not only effective combating of bribery but also comparable levels of enforcement by signatory countries.

Major issues and discrepancies highlighted in 2001 concern: available defenses under some penal law systems, the responsibility of legal persons, effectiveness of sanctions (imprisonment and monetary sanctions), effectiveness of jurisdiction, length of the statute of limitation, accounting and auditing standards[12]. Work is in progress by the Group as to the financing of parties and candidates (which is at the borderline between lawful political activity and illegal bribery), offshore centres' role in facilitating money laundering of bribery (in connection with other OECD bodies focusing on the more general issue), and the coverage of subsidiaries in non-signatory countries (as conduit for multinational com-panies based in signatory countries evading their obligations). This highlights some weak points of the Convention, where completion through protocols, extensive interpretation of obligations, and the expansion of jurisdiction would be desirable in order to avoid circumvention and ineffectiveness.

FOOTNOTES

1   See C. Yannaca Small, "Les paiements illicites dans le commerce international et les actions entreprises pour les combattre", AFDI 1994, p. 792 ff. ; F. Cavalerie, "La Convention de l'OCDE de 1997", *ibid*, 1998, p. 609 ff.

2   Another major achievement of the WG in co-operation with the OECD Committee on Fiscal Affairs was the passing in 1996 of a Recommendation outlawing tax deductibility for bribery payment which in some countries were considered "legitimate business expenses" when paid to foreign public officials.

3   The OECD published the official text of the Convention in a bilingual brochure (English and French) DOC/DAFFE/IME/BR(97) 16, together with the Commentaries (Doc. 17). See also: OECD, "No Longer Business as Usual: Fighting Bribery and Corruption" (contribution by various authors), Paris 2000, p. 276.

4   The fight against corruption in countries which benefit from international multilateral assistance is now being pursued through other means, such as making any aid and assistance conditional upon the reorganization of their administration in accordance with the principle of "good governance"; see World Bank, *Helping countries to combat corruption*, 1997. For the European context, see a communication of the EC Commission *Une politique de l'Union contre la corruption*, COM (97)192 of 21 May 1997.

5   In this perspective, the Convention does not admit any reservations even if this exclusion is mentioned only in the preamble and not in the operative part. No signatory has made a reservation.

6   The US has not been successful in obtaining the support of other countries in order to extend criminalization to include the illicit (corrupt) financing of political parties, a specific case which is regulated differently in different countries and which is not everywhere subject to criminal sanctions. If the granting of a pecuniary advantage to a political party or its officers is the vehicle for corruption in the true sense, it will clearly fall under the Convention. In any case the Group has done further work in this matter, which remains on the agenda.

7   The text does not define "international business transactions", which must be interpreted broadly. Furthermore, according to Article 1 (1), corruption must occur "with a view to obtaining or *retaining* business or other *improper advantage* in the conduct of international business." The text therefore not only covers bribery in transboundary export operations, procurement or investment, but also in contracts and related business, even if it arises only at a later stage (for instance, the bribery by an established foreign investor in order to escape or reduce due taxation).

8   The European Union Convention addresses this question differently in its Art. 6 relating to the "criminal responsibility of company directors". The criminal responsibility of directors or others responsible in the event of acts of corruption "committed by persons subject to their authorities or for the benefit of the company" is provided for. The cases to be covered by the OECD are for all purposes the same.

9   The Working Group held in 1997 a session with prosecutors of several countries (such as France, Switzerland and Italy) in order to learn about the practical difficulties they encounter in investigating bribery cases with an international dimension. A direct result of these contacts is Art. 9.3 of the Convention: "A party shall not decline to render mutual assistance for criminal matters within the scope of this Convention on the ground of bank secrecy".

10 The text of all countries examinations is available on the OECD web site. As the latest Report indicates Brazil, Chile and Turkey have ratified the Convention but have enacted no implementing legislation "and are requested to do so as a matter of urgency".

11 The U.K. adopted implementing legislation as recommended by the Group through the Anti-Terrorism Law adopted in early 2002 in the wake of the September 11, 2001, terrorist attacks in the US.

12 See the Report by the Secretariat, doc BR (2001) 9.

5

Transnational public policy in international arbitral decision-making:
The cases of bribery, money laundering and fraud

By Bernardo M. Cremades

Senior Partner, B. Cremades y Asociados, Madrid, Spain;

Council Member, ICC Institute of World Business Law

and

David J. A. Cairns

Associate, B. Cremades y Asociados, Madrid, Spain

1.   FOUR CONTEMPORARY PROBLEMS

In *Westacre v Jugoimport,* pursuant to a consultancy agreement, Westacre was to receive substantial commissions on any contracts for the sale of military equipment between the Respondents and the Kuwaiti Ministry of Defence. There was a sale contract of substantial value, but the Respondents repudiated the consultancy agreement and refused to pay the commission. Westacre commenced ICC arbitration in Geneva, in accordance with the terms of the dispute resolution clause in the consultancy agreement.

At the hearing, and without any prior reference to such a defence in its pleadings, the Respondents alleged that the agreement was contrary to international public policy and therefore void because Westacre had bribed persons in Kuwait to exercise their influence in favour of the sales contract. The majority of the Arbitral Tribunal found that the bribery was not proven. The majority stated that bribery must be clearly and unequivocally pleaded, that the burden of proof rested firmly on the party making the bribery allegation and that where bribery is not made an issue by the parties, the arbitral tribunal has no duty to investigate possible bribery[1].

The Respondents sought to set the award aside pursuant to Article 190(2)(e) of the Swiss Private International Law Act 1987 on the grounds that the award was incompatible with international public policy. The Respondents further specifically raised the issue of bribery before the Swiss Federal Court. The Federal Court rejected the "… feckless criticism of the arbitral tribunal's findings of fact…" and upheld the award.

The Claimant then sought to enforce the award in England. The Respondents resisted on the grounds that enforcement would be contrary to public policy. The English Court of Appeal faced the question of whether, at the enforcement stage, an English court should investigate the allegations of bribery. The judges of the Court of Appeal could not agree. The majority found that the allegation of bribery has been "… made, entertained and rejected…" by the Arbitral Tribunal, and so there was no justification for re-litigating the issue at the enforcement stage. The dissenting judge (Waller L.J.) saw the issue in terms of competing public policies: on the one hand, of upholding the finality of arbitral awards and, on the other, of ensuring that the English courts did not lend their assistance to an illegal and objectionable contract. He referred to a statement of the trial judge that commercial corruption stood at a different level of opprobrium from a crime such as drug trafficking, and so enforcement should be favoured. Waller L.J. stated:

> "I have reached a different conclusion to that of the judge. I disagree with him as to the appropriate level of opprobrium at which to place commercial corruption. It seems to me that the principle against enforcing a corrupt bargain of the nature of this agreement, … [is] based on public policy of the greatest importance and almost certainly recognised in most jurisdictions throughout the world. I believe it important that the English court is not seen to be turning a blind eye to corruption on this scale ….
>
> The fact is that the arbitrators simply did not have an opportunity of considering the case as now made, and whatever their suspicions, the majority did not feel it in their place to make inquiries ….
>
> The answer is that so far as public policy is concerned it is always unattractive for one party to be able to take the point, but the English court is concerned with the integrity of its own system, and concerned that its executive power is not abused. If the agreement represented a contract to pay a bribe, Westacre should not be entitled to enforce the agreement before an English court and should not be entitled to enforce an award based on it."

The *Westacre* arbitration[2] raises four pressing problems for the international arbitral community relating to corruption and those basic notions of justice and morality that, in the affairs of nations, are collectively described as "public policy." These four problems, which will be examined in this paper, are:

1. In public policy terms, how serious are bribery and corruption? Are they an evil comparable, for example, with drug trafficking or are they a lesser white-collar crime comparable, for example, to tax evasion?

2. Are bribery and corruption matters domestic tribunals can safely entrust to private arbitral tribunals or should domestic courts satisfy themselves independently, at the enforcement stage, that allegations of bribery and corruption are without substance?

3. Does an arbitral tribunal have a duty to investigate possible corruption?

4. If arbitral tribunals do have a duty to investigate possible corruption, then what are the limits of this duty?

The same questions can be posed in respect of both money laundering and accounting fraud, which will also be considered in this paper. By way of preliminary definitions, bribery might be described as the offering, promising or giving of any undue pecuniary or other advantage, whether directly or through intermediaries, to a foreign public official in order to obtain or retain business; money laundering is the concealment or transfer of profits derived from the commission of a crime so as to disguise its true nature, source or ownership. Fraud is a very general concept, but is limited in this paper to accounting fraud, and in particular the falsification or destruction of business records for an illegal purpose[3].

2. THE CURRENT PUBLIC POLICY SIGNIFICANCE OF CORRUPTION, MONEY LAUNDERING AND FRAUD

As recognised by Article 35 of the ICC Rules of Arbitration, an arbitrator has an obligation to make every effort to make sure the award is enforceable at law. This obligation means that arbitrators must have regard to the international public policy of States that might be related to the parties, the contract or the enforcement of the award, because a breach of public policy is a ground under Article V.2(b) of the New York Convention 1958 for a domestic court to refuse to recognise or enforce an arbitral award. The globalisation of the international economy is increasing the significance and altering the content of international public policy, most fundamentally by requiring attention to new international norms relating to the protection of human rights, the environment and cultural sites[4]. The increasing integration of world markets has also raised the profile and prompted sustained international action in respect of corruption, money laundering and fraud. The developments in international rule-making in these areas over the last decades or so have both been impressive and attracted a broad base of support, particularly amongst capital-exporting nations. There is no doubt today that corruption and money laundering are not to be tolerated or condoned in international commerce or that the suppression of corruption and money laundering is an established part of international public policy to which international arbitrators must have regard. The place of fraud in inter-national public policy is complicated by difficulties in definition, but certainly some manifestations of fraud, particularly those that might conceal illegal activities such as corruption and money laundering, are without doubt prescribed by international public policy.

a)   Bribery and corruption

The modern public policy significance of bribery and corruption can be traced back to concerns in the mid-1970s regarding the means by which multinationals obtained contracts abroad. This concern, fueled by scandals involving the bribery of foreign government officials by US business, prompted the United States to enact the Foreign Corrupt Practices Act in 1977. The purpose of the FCPA was to prevent the bribery of foreign officials and to restore public confidence in the integrity of US business and for this purpose made it an offence to make corrupt payments to foreign public officials in order to obtain or keep business. In the same year, an International Chamber of Commerce committee, under the Chairman-ship of Lord Shawcross, urged co-ordinated international action, including self-regulation by business, to combat bribery and extortion. To assist self-regulation by business, the committee produced the first version of what are now known as the *ICC Rules of Conduct: Extortion and Bribery in International Business Transactions*.[5]

The impetus for the elevation of the US' measure into an inter-national standard came from the distortive effects of corruption on competition. The restrictions imposed by the FCPA placed US business at a competitive disadvantage compared with foreign companies that routinely paid bribes and, in some countries, even were able to claim bribes as deductible expenses for tax purposes. Accordingly, the United States pressed for parallel legislation from its trading partners. During the 1990s, there was a flurry of international initiatives against bribery and corruption, culminating in *1997 OECD Convention on Combating Bribery of Foreign Public Officials* (hereafter the "OECD Bribery Convention"). The initiatives of the 1990s are well summarised by an International Monetary Fund report on the OECD Bribery Convention.

> "... the *OECD Bribery Convention* benefited from a favourable international climate in which several other international anti-corruption initiatives came to fruition. The Inter-American Convention Against Corruption organized by the Organization of American States ... was opened for ratification in 1996. A World Trade Organization ... Ministerial Conference launched in 1996 a study on transparency in government procurement practices. The European Union ... approved a convention on combating corruption in 1997, and the Council of Europe ... finalized a regional anti-corruption convention in 1999. The United Nations ... General Assembly adopted a resolution in 1997 requesting the Secretary General to assist member states in designing strategies to prevent and control corruption, which has since become a priority for the United Nations Development Program.... The World Bank in its *World Development Report 1997: The State in a Changing World* laid out an agenda for prompting good governance.... Transparency International, the leading NGO in anti-corruption, was launched in 1994, and in 1996 the International Chamber of Commerce adopted *Extortion and Bribery in International Business Transactions-Rules and Recommendations*"[6].

The OECD Bribery Convention requires the signatory States to establish bribery of a foreign public official as a criminal offence under their national laws. The offence is defined in Article 1 of the Convention, which includes a definition of "foreign public official". The Convention requires signatories to criminalize practices that might facilitate the commission or concealment of bribery under their money laundering and accounting legislation, and to commit themselves to mutual legal assistance and either to extradite or prosecute their nationals accused of the bribery of a foreign public official. The application of the OECD Bribery Convention is limited in that it requires signatories to criminalize only the offering or paying of bribes, and not the soliciting or receiving of bribes, and covers only public officials, and not private agents, employees or corporate officers. As at October 10, 2002, 34 countries had enacted national legislation to implement the OECD Bribery Convention[7].

The rapid and widespread promotion of anti-bribery and anti-corruption norms by various intergovernmental organisations (IGOs) has been described as a "norm cascade"[8]. International rule-making has been complemented by the work of non-governmental organisations (NGOs) such as the International Chamber of Commerce, referred to in the above quotation, and Transparency International which have highlighted the problems of bribery and corruption and encouraged business to address them[9]. Transparency International publishes annual Corruption Indices. These indices include the Corruption Perceptions Index which identifies the countries where corruption is most prevalent, and the Bribe Payers Index, which identifies the propensity of companies from leading export countries to pay bribes to senior public officials and also identifies the business sectors where bribery and corruption are most prevalent. It is significant that the three international business sectors where the perceptions of corruption are highest – public works and construction, arms and defence and oil and gas – are sectors of major importance for international commercial arbitration[10].

b) Money laundering

(i) Nature of money laundering: The essence of money laundering is processing the proceeds of crime to disguise their illegal origin. It typically involves three stages:

- *placement* of the criminal proceeds in the financial system;
- *layering* or engaging in a series of movements or conversions of the proceeds to distance them from their source;

and finally

- *integration* of the proceeds into a legitimate economy.

(ii) Criminalisation of money laundering: Money laundering has experienced a rapid rise in its international profile since the term was first coined in the 1970s. The catalyst for the development of international rules relating to money laundering has been its intimate connection with the activities of organised crime and particularly drug trafficking. A major advance in the prohibition and punishment of money laundering was achieved in 1988 at Vienna with the *United Nations Convention Against Illicit Traffic in Narcotic Drug and Psychotropic Substances* (hereafter the "Vienna Convention"). Article 3 of the "Vienna Convention" requires signatories to criminalize any dealings in property derived from drug offences, including the following dealings:

"1.Each Party shall adopt such measures as may be necessary to establish

as criminal offences under its domestic law, when committed intentionally:
a)…

b)(i) The conversion or transfer of property, knowing that such property is derived from a [drug-related] offence or offences, or from an act of participation in such offences or offences, for the purpose of concealing or disguising the illicit origin of the property or of assisting any person who is involved in the commission of such an offence or offences to evade the legal consequences of his actions;

(ii) The concealment or disguise of the true nature, source, location, disposition, movement, rights with respect to, or ownership of property, knowing that such property is derived from a [drug-related] offence or offences, or from an act of participation in such an offence or offences;

c) Subject to its constitutional principles and the basic concepts of its legal system:

(i) The acquisition, possession or use of property, knowing, at the time of receipt, that such property was derived from a [drug-related] offence or offences, or from an act of participation in such offence or offences;…."

Article 3 of the Vienna Convention has served as the template for the definitions of money laundering in subsequent international instruments such as the Council of Europe's Convention on Laundering, Search, Seizure and Confiscation of the Proceeds of Crime in 1990, the European Directive on Prevention of the Use of the Financial System for the Purpose of Money Laundering in 1991 (hereafter the "1991 European Directive") and the United Nations Convention against Transnational Organized Crime in 2001[11].

It was the Financial Action Task Force on Money Laundering (hereafter FATF) that took up the challenge of extending the international prohibition of money laundering from the proceeds of drug offences to the proceeds of any serious crime. The FATF is an IGO established by the 1989 G7 Summit in Paris. Twenty-nine countries and two international organisations (the European Commission and the Gulf Co-operation Council) are members of the FATF. The mandate of the FATF includes the development and promotion of policies, at national and international levels, to combat money laundering and to monitor members' progress in implementing anti-money laundering measures. Its main achievement to date is the Forty Recommendations drawn up in 1990 and reviewed in 1996, which set out measures that members and all other countries are encouraged to adopt. The Forty Recommendations require countries to ratify and implement fully the Vienna Convention (Recommendation 1) and in Recommendations 4 to 6 advocate the extension of the definition of money laundering in the Vienna Convention to all "serious offences":

> "Scope of the Criminal Offence of Money laundering
>
> 4. Each country should take such measures as may be necessary, including legislative ones, to enable it to criminalize money laundering as set forth in the Vienna Convention. Each country should extend the offence of drug money laundering to one based on serious offences. Each country would determine which serious crimes would be designated as money laundering predicate offences.
>
> 5. As provided in the Vienna Convention, the offence of money laundering should apply as least to knowing money laundering activity, including the concept that knowledge may be inferred form objective factual circumstances.
>
> 6. Where possible, corporations themselves – not only their employees – should be subject to criminal liability."

The widespread criminalization of money laundering for serious offences has today firmly established money laundering as an international crime.

(iii) Financial system regulation in combating money laundering: The FATF also sought to extend the framework of anti-money laundering efforts from the criminalization of money laundering to the regulation of the institutions through which money might be laundered. Recommendations 8 to 29 of the Forty Recommendations addressed the role of the financial system in combating money laundering, covering such matters as customer identification and record keeping, the need for financial institutions to develop programmes against money laundering and the need for increased diligence by financial institutions when dealing with complex transactions or unusual patterns of transactions, including the need to report suspicions to competent authorities[12].

During the decade of the 1990s, there was a comprehensive wave of rule-making initiatives directed at money laundering from the United Nations, the European Union and the Organisation of American States, national legislatures, specialist IGOs in the banking sector and from the private banking sector. Of particular significance was the 1991 European Directive, which required Member States to impose customer identification requirements on financial and credit institutions to ensure these institutions examined "… with special attention any transaction which they regard as particularly likely, by its nature, to be related to money laundering …", and that they established adequate internal control procedures to forestall and prevent money laundering. Two features of 1991 European Directive anticipated the further expansion of regulatory measures against money laundering.

Firstly, Article 6 of the 1991 European Directive anticipated the development of a disclosure or "whistleblowing" obligation whereby credit and financial institutions, their directors and employees might be required to disclose suspicious transactions to authorities. Article 6 provides:

"**Article 6**
Member States shall ensure that credit and financial institutions and their directors and employees co-operate fully with the authorities responsible for combating money laundering:

■ by informing those authorities, on their own initiative, of any fact which might be an indication of money laundering,

■ by furnishing those authorities, at their request, with all necessary information, in accordance with the procedures established by the applicable legislation…."

The creation of a whistleblowing obligation in respect of money laundering required the modification of established standards of banking secrecy. Accordingly, Article 9 of the 1991 European Directive provides:

"**Article 9**
The disclosure in good faith to the authorities responsible for combating money laundering by an employee or director of a credit or financial institution of the information … shall not constitute a breach of any restriction on disclosure of information imposed by contract or by any legislative, regulatory or administrative provision, and shall not involve the credit or financial institution, its directors or employees in liability of any kind."

Secondly, the recitals of 1991 European Directive recognised that:

"... since money laundering can be carried out not only through credit and financial institutions but also through other types of professions and categories of undertakings, Member States must extend the provisions of this Directive in whole or in part, to include those professions and undertakings whose activities are particularly likely to be used for money laundering purposes."

The legal and accounting professions are particularly susceptible to involvement in the facilitation of money laundering. In general, Europe's legal professions have resisted the extension to their activities of client identification, internal controls, and suspicious-transaction reporting requirements, raising objections of client confidentiality and legal professional privilege[13]. However, the Second Directive on Money Laundering of 2001 (with which Member States are required to comply by June 15, 2003) now requires Member States to extend money laundering regulations to the legal professions, but preserves the legal profession's privilege in respect of the defence of clients in legal proceedings. The compromise adopted by the European Union is set out in the recitals to the Second Directive[14]:

"... (15) The obligations of the Directive concerning customer identification, record keeping and the reporting of suspicious transactions should be extended to a limited number of activities and professions which have been shown to be vulnerable to money laundering.

(16) Notaries and independent legal professionals, as defined by the Member States, should be made subject to the provisions of the Directive when participating in financial or corporate transactions, including providing tax advice....

(17) However, where independent members of professions providing legal advice which are legally recognised and controlled, such as lawyers, are ascertaining the legal position of a client or representing a client in legal proceedings, it would not be appropriate under the Directive to put these legal professionals in respect of these activities under an obligation to report suspicions of money laundering. There must be exemptions from any obligation to report information obtained either before, during or after judicial proceedings, or in the course of ascertaining the legal position for a client. Thus, legal advice remains subject to the obligation of professional secrecy unless the legal counsellor is taking part in money laundering

activities, the legal advice is provided for money laundering purposes, or the lawyer knows that the client is seeking legal advice for money laundering purposes."

Accordingly, the legal professional privilege, and more generally the right to a fair trial guaranteed by the European Convention on Human Rights and similar instruments, will mark a limit to any obligation of legal advisers to disclose suspicious transactions that might involve money laundering.

(iv) Private sector initiatives: Perhaps the most significant initiative in the private sector has been the *Global Anti Money-Laundering Guidelines for Private Banking* (hereafter the "Wolfsberg AML Principles"). The "Wolfsberg AML Principles" were promulgated by a group of leading banks, with the participation of Transparency International, in a voluntary effort to control money laundering and to establish a common global standard for their private banking operations. The "Wolfsberg AML Principles" include due diligence provisions relating to client identification and identity categories of persons requiring additional diligence, provisions for identifying unusual or suspicious transactions, and monitoring, control and reporting in relation to money laundering. The classes of persons requiring additional diligence are defined as follows[15]:

> **"2.   Client acceptance: situations requiring additional diligence/ attention**
>
> **2.1. General**
>
> In its internal policies, the bank must define categories of persons whose circumstances warrant additional diligence. This will typically be the case where the circumstances are likely to pose a higher than average risk to a bank.
>
> **2.2. Indicators**
>
> The circumstances of the following categories of persons are indicators for defining them as requiring additional diligence:
>
> – Persons residing in and/or having funds sourced from countries identified by credible sources as having inadequate anti-money laundering standards or representing high risk for crime and corruption.
> – Persons engaged in types of business activities or sectors known to be susceptible to money laundering.
> – "Politically Exposed Persons"(frequently abbreviated as "PEPs"), referring

to individuals holding or having held positions of public trust, such as governmental officials, senior executives of government corporations, politicians, important political party officials, etc., as well as their families and close associates."

(v) Organised crime and terrorism: It is clear, however, that the prevention of money laundering is not simply or primarily an issue of banking or financial regulation; it is a major priority in the fight against organised crime. Money laundering has a prominent place in the recent United Nations Convention Against Transnational Organized Crime[16] and recent national legislation such as the Proceeds of Crimes Act 2002 (UK)[17]. The September 11, 2001 attacks on the World Trade Center have emphasized the link between money laundering and terrorism and given further urgency to its criminalization. The United States included anti-money laundering amendments in the USA Patriot Act enacted in October 2001[18]. Leading IGOs have also addressed money laundering and terrorist financing. The FATF issued Special Recommendations on Terrorist Financing on October 31, 2001 and the Basel Committee on Banking Supervision has lent its support to collective action to identify and halt terrorist financing[19].

c) Fraud

Accounting practices are a highly technical field more susceptible to national legislation then international regulation, so it is perhaps not surprising that fraud has not witnessed the same degree of international co-operation and rule-making as corruption and money laundering. However, fraudulent record-keeping facilitates and helps to conceal corruption, money laundering and other crime, particularly securities fraud. For this reason, the OECD Bribery Convention includes an article requiring Signatories to ensure that companies keep complete and accurate financial records, and particularly targets off-the-books or secret accounts or transactions, non-existent or mis-described expenditures and the use of false documentation. It also requires Signatories to adequately punish "…omissions and falsifications in respect of the books, records, accounts and financial statements of such companies…."[20]. The European Union has sought to harmonise the financial information presented by publicly-traded companies to ensure a high degree of transparency and compatibility of financial statements by endorsing in 2002 the international accounting standards adopted by the International Accounting Standards Board[21]. A wave of recent corporate collapses, primarily in the United States and involving massive losses for creditors, investors and employees, has focussed attention on fraudulent accounting practices and led the United States to enact the Sarbanes-Oxley Act of 2002, with the intention of improving the quality and transparency of financial reporting, independent audits and accounting services for public companies. The Sarbanes-Oxley Act includes a limited "whistleblower" obligation imposed on lawyers, who are required to report any "...evidence of material violation of securities law or breach of fiduciary duty or similar violation..." by the company or its agents to the General Counsel or Chief Executive Officer and, in some circumstances, to its full Board of Directors.

d)   Conclusions

This brief survey of international developments demonstrates that bribery of a foreign public official and money laundering are now serious crimes in international law. They can no longer be considered as simply as reprehensible business practices, or unavoidable evils of doing business in difficult parts of the world. Bribery and money laundering have been widely and repeatedly condemned by the international community.

Bribery, corruption and fraud also undermine the integrity of international business and create dangerous links between business and organized crime. They have pernicious macro-economic effects, including the distortion of competition and securities markets and help to perpetuate the power of corrupt regimes in developing countries, and so indirectly contribute to retarded economic development and human rights abuses. A recent World Bank report identified the "...large costs..." of corruption for economic development as including less competition, less foreign direct investment, lower tax revenues, lower public spending on health and education and a loss of legitimacy of the state with a consequent loss of capacity to provide institutions that support markets[22].

The banking sector has had to accept limitations on its established principles of confidentiality and to report suspicion transactions. The legal profession is also going to have to accept disclosure obligations in respect of transactions that might involve money laundering, subject to the protection of legal professional privilege where the right of defence of the client is involved. Lawyers in the US also have limited disclosure obligations in respect of fraudulent accounting. It is clear, therefore, that the public policy concerns relating to money laundering and, to a lesser extent, fraud, are sufficiently strong to override the traditional professional confidentiality between lawyers and clients in some circumstances.

Accordingly, there is no doubt today that the suppression of corruption and money laundering is an established part of international public policy and must be respected by international arbitrators. The place of fraud in international public policy is more complex, but certainly some manifestations of fraud, particularly those that might conceal corruption and money laundering or serious crime, are also proscribed by international public policy.

3. THE ENFORCEMENT OF ARBITRAL AWARDS INVOLVING CONTRACTS TAINTED WITH CORRUPTION, MONEY LAUNDERING OR FRAUD

If we return to the *Westacre* arbitration, we can see that Waller L.J. was correct when he said that the "…principle against enforcing a corrupt bargain…[is] based on public policy of the greatest importance and almost certainly recognised in most jurisdictions throughout the world…." A similar conclusion is likely to be drawn by tribunals in most jurisdictions, in respect not only of contracts tainted with corruption, but also contracts involving an element of money laundering.

The international public policy significance of bribery of a foreign public official and money laundering means that an award that does not adequately address issues of this nature arising in the course of the arbitration is liable either to be set aside by the tribunals of the jurisdiction where the award was made or refused recognition and enforcement in jurisdictions where enforcement might subsequently be sought. The fact that an award conflicts with the public policy of the seat of the arbitration is normally sufficient under applicable national laws to justify that it be set aside by the tribunals of that place[23]. Similarly, pursuant to Article V.2.b of the New York Convention[24], enforcement tribunals are justified in refusing to recognise and enforce awards relating to contracts tainted with bribery of a foreign public official or money laundering.

However, as the history of the *Westacre* arbitration confirms, the courts at the seat of the arbitration and at the place of enforcement must also bear in mind the public policy interest in respecting the proper jurisdiction of arbitral tribunals and upholding the finality of arbitral awards. If a contract involves elements of bribery or money laundering, then the arbitral tribunal is the forum to evaluate the evidence and determine the implications of the bribery and money laundering for the claims and defences of the parties, under the contract and the applicable law. In practical terms, therefore, a court hearing an application for setting aside or for recognition and enforcement is much more likely to uphold an award, or to recognise and enforce an award, notwithstanding bribery or money laundering, where the issues of bribery or money laundering have been acknowledged and dealt with in the award by the arbitral tribunal.

In general terms, the position is the same in respect of fraud, with the caveat that the public policy imperative to refuse to uphold or enforce an award relating to a contract tainted with accounting fraud is weaker where there is no evidence that the fraud involves corruption, money laundering or other serious crime.

4.   THE OBLIGATION OF AN ARBITRAL TRIBUNAL TO INVESTIGATE CORRUPTION, MONEY LAUNDERING AND FRAUD

From the above analysis, it follows that when an allegation of bribery of a foreign public official, money laundering, or fraud involving a serious offence is raised before an arbitral tribunal, then the arbitral tribunal should:

a) recognise the public policy significance of the allegation;

b) fully investigate the evidence relating to the allegation and determine its significance under the applicable law; and

c) explicitly refer to the allegation and its factual and legal conclusions relating to the allegation in its award.

The explicit allegation of bribery, money laundering or serious fraud is, however, only the most obvious case. The allegation might not be explicitly made by either party, but, rather, enter into the arbitration by suspicion or innuendo as the proceedings progress, or the parties might acknowledge an element of corruption, money laundering or fraud, but ask that the arbitral tribunal ignore it in deciding the dispute before it. This latter situation occurred in perhaps the most well known arbitral award dealing with bribery of foreign public officials, that of Judge Lagergren in ICC Case No. 1110, decided in 1963. The arbitration involved a claim for commissions by an Argentinian agent in respect of public works contracts awarded by the Perón regime in Argentina to the Respondent. It was acknowledged by the General Manager of the Respondent that large commissions were required for the purpose of bribing government officials and that "…anybody who had any dealing in the Argentine, one way or the other, had to face this condition….." Both parties confirmed that they considered the agency contract binding and effective and asked the tribunal to decide their case in accordance with the terms of reference. Judge Lagergren decided that he could not just ignore the issue of bribery and so examined it on his own motion[25].

The decision of Judge Lagergren was ahead of its time. Whatever the position might have been in 1963, it is clear today that an arbitral tribunal has a duty to examine any corruption, money laundering or serious fraud occurring in the negotiation or performance of the contract, even if the parties do not wish it to do so. The assertion made in the *Westacre* arbitration that an arbitral tribunal has no duty to investigate bribery unless one of the parties explicitly raises the issue is incompatible with the modern significance of bribery in international public policy[26].

There are four clear reasons why an arbitral tribunal must investigate bribery of a foreign public official, money laundering or serious fraud irrespective of the wishes of the parties. Firstly, an arbitral tribunal has a duty, as confirmed by Article 35 of the ICC Rules of Arbitration, to make every effort to ensure its award is enforceable in law, and any award that ignores evidence of bribery, money laundering or serious fraud carries a significant risk of subsequently being held to be contrary to public policy and therefore unenforceable. Secondly, and notwithstanding the private and often confidential nature of international arbitration, arbitral tribunals have a public responsibility to the administration of justice that is inseparable from their autonomy as recognised and respected by national courts. In fact, the public responsibilities of international arbitral tribunals are rapidly growing in prominence. This public responsibility requires arbitral tribunals not to condone bribery, money laundering or serious fraud[27]. Thirdly, international arbitration is a service provided to States and businesses engaged in international trade and investment, and a proactive approach by international arbitrators best assists the considerable efforts States and businesses are making to develop and implement rules and systems to eliminate bribery and money laundering. Finally, weak or apathetic judicial authorities have been identified as one of the root causes of the persistence of corruption[28], and it is in the interests of the international arbitration community as a whole to assist actively in the elimination of corruption rather than risk being seen as a weak and complicit aid to its survival.

Possible bribery of a foreign public official, money laundering or fraud must no longer be discreetly ignored by lawyers and arbitrators on the basis that such practices are an inevitable part of doing business in less developed regions of the world. Where a dispute arises and an arbitral tribunal is appointed, the parties expect the tribunal to know and understand trade practices in the industry and the region concerned, but they have no right to expect arbitrators to ignore either the applicable law or international public policy. Bribery, money laundering and fraud are not issues of moral choice for an arbitrator. They involve crimes, widely condemned in the international community, which under no circumstances must be condoned or facilitated by a reluctance of arbitral tribunals to recognise the true nature of these acts.

There are now substantial sources of information available to enable arbitral tribunals to identify the warning signs or "red flags" of bribery, money laundering and serious fraud that justify further investigation or questioning of the parties or their witnesses. The business sectors and countries particularly afflicted by corruption are well publicised; certain characteristics of commission or agency contracts – including unusual payment patterns, disproportionate commissions, ill-defined services, and the character of the relationship between the agent and a foreign public official – might indicate bribery if no alternative explanation is forthcoming[29], and the establishment of off-the-books accounts, the making of off-the-books or inadequately identified transactions, the recording of non-existent expenditures, the entry of liabilities with incorrect identification of their purpose, as well as the use of false documents, appear in the OECD Bribery Convention as possible indications of bribery[30]. A multinational today should possess a policy and code of conduct on bribery and, if it does, a copy may be requested by the arbitral tribunal and then used as a basis of enquiries designed to test compliance in respect of the specific transaction at issue. Similarly, the techniques commonly employed to launder money – at least outside the specialist banking sector – and the types of transactions and persons that create suspicions of money laundering – payments in cash, suspiciously named accounts, use of offshore companies, large deposits and transfers, use of professional facilitators such as lawyers and accountants and the involvement of "politically exposed persons" – should be familiar to international arbitrators[31].

This does not, of course, mean that every suspicious element in the execution or performance of the contract should set the tribunal off on an inquisitorial exercise of its own irrespective of the wishes of the parties. Where suspicious circumstances exist, the tribunal's duty is not to ignore its suspicions, but to seek an explanation from the parties. A tribunal concerned, for example, by the remuneration arrangements for a foreign agent can seek an explanation of those arrangements without suggesting they might have a corrupt purpose. A discreet request for further information, if properly used, should enable an arbitral tribunal to either eliminate a suspicion of illegal activity or to confirm the need for the possibility of bribery, money laundering or serious fraud to be raised explicitly with the parties.

The arbitral tribunal should be suspicious of requests for awards by consent in respect of transactions that might involve bribery, fraud and, particularly, money laundering. Money might in fact be laundered through the presentation of a contrived dispute to arbitration in order to obtain a legitimate award that is then used to assist the defendant in laundering money through the payment of damages to the claimant[32]. The parties might wish to avoid inquiries by the arbitral tribunal into the legality of their conduct by terminating the arbitration. This the parties are entitled to do, but the tribunal should not assist them by making an award by consent. The discretion of an arbitral tribunal to refuse to make an award by consent jointly requested by both parties has been authoritatively examined and approved in the context of the drafting of the UNCITRAL Model Law and by the Iran-United States Claims Tribunal[33].

The actual effect of bribery, money laundering or serious fraud on the rights and duties of the parties to a contract depends upon the facts of the case and the applicable law. Judge Lagergren found that the effect of the corruption in the case before him was to deny jurisdiction to the tribunal, but this reasoning has been criticised for failing to recognise the separability of the contract and the arbitration agreement, and the fact that the arbitration agreement itself is unlikely to be tainted with corruption[34]. This issue is beyond the scope of this paper, but whether proven bribery, money laundering or serious fraud are dealt with as an issue of jurisdiction or as an issue of the merits under the applicable law, there is no doubt that an arbitral tribunal must condemn conduct so plainly contrary to international public policy.

5. LIMITS OF AN ARBITRAL TRIBUNAL'S DUTY TO INVESTIGATE POSSIBLE BRIBERY OF A PUBLIC OFFICIAL, MONEY LAUNDERING AND FRAUD

The most difficult question arising from the modern public policy significance of bribery of a foreign public official, money laundering or fraud is that of the proper limits of an arbitral tribunal's duty to investigate this conduct. Where neither party explicitly alleges bribery, money laundering or fraud, the threshold for an arbitral tribunal to seek further information and begin an investigation on its own initiative is obviously a high one and would require strong suspicions of illegal activities. However, if this threshold is reached or if one of the parties alleges bribery, money laundering or fraud and therefore requires the tribunal to investigate the possibility that such activities have occurred, then the following considerations might guide the tribunal's investigation:

a) The primacy of due process/natural justice

Bribery, money laundering and fraud are serious crimes and, even when investigated in the private adjudicative context of arbitration, must be approached with procedural safeguards commensurate with the gravity of the allegations. The party or parties suspected of bribery, money laundering or fraud must be fully informed of the tribunal's suspicions and allowed the time and opportunity to make a full response. They are entitled to know the bases of the allegations against them and should be granted an oral hearing if they so request.

The seriousness of the allegations means that the burden of proof, as the *Westacre* ICC tribunal acknowledged, is highly important[35]. The burden of proof is clearly on the party making the allegation of bribery, money laundering or fraud and the proof should be convincing. Uncorroborated evidence or evidence capable of multiple explanations should normally be rejected. If the demonstration of the party alleging bribery is not convincing, the arbitral tribunal in ICC Case 6497 of 1994 stated, then "…the tribunal should reject its argument, even if the tribunal has some doubts about the possible bribery nature of the agreements." [36]

b) Examination of only the enforceability of the contract in dispute

The arbitral tribunal is established as a private adjudicator for a contractual dispute between two parties and its public policy duty is restricted to ensuring that this contract is not illegal or unenforceable by reason of bribery, money laundering or fraud. The tribunal should not investigate or allow a party to adduce evidence relating to other contracts, transactions or activities of one of the other parties or their representatives. It should firmly reject the argument that illegal activities in other contracts or circumstances are evidence that similar conduct taints the contract in dispute.

Any award that makes findings in relation to bribery, money laundering and fraud that go beyond the issue of the validity or enforceability or the contract in dispute risks being set aside on the grounds of being *ultra petita*.

c) Alertness to the tactical abuse of allegations of bribery, money laundering or fraud

The tribunal must guard against the tactical use of allegations to avoid making payments as previously agreed, or to otherwise deflect attention from one party's own contractual non-performance. The *Westacre* arbitration demonstrates that corruption is an easy allegation to make, but difficult to prove or disprove. Influence does not necessarily indicate bribery, concealment of the sources of funds should not automatically be equated with money laundering, and departures from normal accounting practices are not always evidence of fraud.

d) Confidentiality

It might be appropriate for the arbitral tribunal to consider special orders relating to the confidentiality of the arbitration while allegations of bribery, money laundering and fraud are under investigation.

e) Privilege

As bribery, money laundering and fraud involve criminal activities, parties might invoke legal professional privilege or, in some jurisdictions, the privilege against self-incrimination, in rejecting requests from the arbitral tribunal for further information. In certain circumstances, a negative inference may be drawn from a refusal to disclose information, but given the seriousness of the allegations, such inferences must be drawn with care.

f) No duty of disclosure

Finally, there is the question of whether under any circumstances an arbitral tribunal might have a duty to disclose its award to regulatory authorities of any jurisdiction where criminal activity might have occurred. The emergence of "whistleblowing" obligations in respect of money laundering and fraud in some jurisdictions has already been noted.

Such duty could only arise from express legislation in a jurisdiction to which the arbitral tribunal, or some of its members, were subject. The writers are not aware of any such legislation, and there would appear to be strong public policy objections to it. The imposition of an obligation on arbitrators to disclose possible bribery, money laundering or fraud that comes to their notice in the course of an arbitration might compromise the right to a fair and independent determination of civil rights guaranteed by Article 6 of the European Convention On Human Rights.

6.   CONCLUSIONS

The arbitral tribunal is appointed by the parties themselves to resolve a dispute between them. There is no doubt that indications of bribery of a foreign public official, money laundering or serious fraud complicate the relationship of the arbitral tribunal with the parties and makes its engagement much more difficult to perform. Allegations of bribery, money laundering or serious fraud will always evince a strong response from the other party, whether it be indignant denial or a barrage of counter-allegations of wrongdoing. The tribunal has to proceed with care, and its task is not made easier by the risk that a party may reveal the corrupt purpose of a contract in order to avoid sharing its benefits with the other party[37] or otherwise to escape the consequences of its own contractual non-performance.

The most difficult situation for an arbitral tribunal is where the tribunal itself suspects bribery of a foreign public official, money laundering or serious fraud, but this illegality is not raised by either of the parties in its pleadings or the tribunal is informed that the parties consider the bribery, money laundering or serious fraud to be merely incidental and are united in their wish that the arbitral tribunal disregard it in deciding the dispute. Notwithstanding the view expressed in some awards that an arbitral tribunal has no duty to address bribery not pleaded by the parties, this position is simply incompatible with the modern significance of bribery of a foreign public official in international public policy. In fact, perhaps the greatest mistake an arbitral tribunal can make when faced with a suspicion of bribery, money laundering or serious fraud is to ignore it; it is much better for the suspicion to be acknowledged and the evidence addressed, even if the conclusion ultimately is that the evidence is inconclusive.

The position today is that the international arbitrator has a clear duty to address issues of bribery, money laundering or serious fraud whenever they arise in the arbitration and whatever the wishes of the parties and to record its legal and factual conclusions in its award. This is the only course available to protect the enforceability of the award and the integrity of the institution of international commercial arbitration.

FOOTNOTES

1   The majority stated: "... In arbitration proceedings, however, bribery is a fact which has to be alleged and for which evidence has to be submitted, and at the same time constitutes a defence, nullifying the claims arising from a contract. The consequences of this are decisive (...).

If a claimant asserts claims arising from a contract, and the defendant objects that the claimant's rights arising from the contract are null due to bribery, it is up to the defendant to present the fact of bribery and the pertaining evidence (...). The statement of facts and the burden of proof are therefore upon the defendant. The word 'bribery' is clear and unmistakable. If the defendant does not use it in his presentation of facts an Arbitral Tribunal does not have to investigate. It is exclusively the parties' presentation of facts that decides in what direction the arbitral tribunal has to investigate (...).

If the claimant's claim based on the contract is to be voided by the defence of bribery, the arbitral tribunal ... must be convinced that there is indeed a case of bribery. A mere 'suspicion' by any member of the arbitral tribunal ... is entirely insufficient...."

2   The description of the *Westacre* arbitration and subsequent litigation is taken from the report of the English Court of Appeal decision in *Westacre Investments Inc v Jugoimport SDRP Holdings*, Court of Appeal, May 12, 1999. This decision, and other recent English decisions on illegality and public policy, are discussed in Ewan Brown, "Illegality and Public Policy – Enforcement of Arbitral Awards in England: *Hilmarton Limited v Omnium de Traitement et de Valorisation S.A."* [2000] *Int. A.L.R.* 31-35.

3   **Corruption:** This description of corruption is broadly consistent with the *Foreign Corrupt Practices Act,* 15 U.S.C. §§78dd *et seq.* and the 1997 *Convention on Combating Bribery of Foreign Public Officials in International Business Transactions.* It should be noted that both this Convention and the *Foreign Corrupt Practices Act* concern only the bribery of foreign *public* officials. Similarly, the discussion of bribery and corruption in this paper relates to public officials. Money Laundering: The definition of money laundering is from the internationally recognised definition of money laundering in Article 1 of the 1988 *United Nations Convention Against Illicit Traffic in Narcotic Drugs and Psychotropic Substances.* This definition refers to the laundering of money derived from drug offences, but as the Forty Recommendations of the Financial Action Task

Force on Money Laundering recognize, the definition can simply be extended from drug offences to any *"serious offences"* (see especially Recommendations 1, 4, 5 and 7). Fraud: Fraud is a general term not capable of comprehensive definition. Discussion in this paper is limited to accountancy fraud.

4   On globalisation and public policy see Bernardo M. Cremades and David J. A. Cairns, "The Brave New World of Global Arbitration" (2002), 3 *Journal of World Investment* 173-209, at 205-208.

5   For the *ICC Rules of Conduct: Extortion and Bribery in International Business Trans-actions* see François Vincke, Fritz Heimann & Ron Katz *Fighting Bribery: A corporate practices manual* (ICC publication 610) [see also *Fighting Corruption: A corporate practices manual* (ICC publication 652)].

6   International Monetary Fund, *OECD Convention on Combating Bribery of Foreign Public Officials in International Business Transactions* (available at: *http://www.imf.org/external/np/gov/2001/eng/091801.htm*) (2001); paragraph 10. This report summarises the background to the OECD Bribery Convention, its principal features and interpretation. For further background on the Foreign Corrupt Practices Act and the OECD Bribery Convention see Kenneth W. Abbott, "Rule Making in the WTO: Lessons from the Case of Bribery and Corruption" (2001) *Journal of International Economic Law,* 275-296 at 275-278; Foreign Corrupt Practices Act Anti Bribery Provisions, U.S. Department of Justice Website: *http://www.usdoj.gov/criminal/fraud/fcpa/dojdocb.htm.* For the text of *the Inter-American Convention Against Corruption* of 1996 see *http://www.oas.org/juridico/english/Treaties/b-58.html.*

7   *Ratification Status As at 10 October 2002,* available on the OECD website at *http://www.oecd.org/pdf/M00017000/M00017037.pdf.*

8   See Kenneth W. Abbott, "Rule Making in the WTO: Lessons from the Case of Bribery and Corruption" (*2001) Journal of International Economic Law,* 275-296 at 278.

9   NGOs like Transparency International are becoming increasingly relevant actors for the international arbitration community: see Bernardo M. Cremades and David J. A. Cairns, "The Brave New World of Global Arbitration" (2002) 3 *Journal of World Investment* 173-209, especially at 178-180 and 197-199.

10 See Robin Hodess (ed.) *Global Corruption Report 2001* (Transparency International, Berlin, 2001) especially at 232 (*2001 Corruption Perceptions Index*) and 237 (*1999 Bribe Payers Index*). The *Bribe Payers Index 2002* is available on Transparency International's web site at http://www.transparency.org/. A recent survey by the consultancy Control Risks Group of companies in the United States, the United Kingdom, Germany, the Netherlands, Hong Kong and Singapore confirms the prevalence of corruption, notwithstanding the international pressures, with 40% of respondents believing they had lost business in the last five years because of competitors' bribes, a figure which rises to 55.8% in the Public Works/Construction sector: see Control Risks Group, *Facing up to Corruption: Survey Results 2002,* available at: *http://www.crg.com/html.*

11 See Article 6 of the Convention on Laundering, Search, Seizure and Confiscation of the Proceeds of Crime, the definition of *"money laundering"* in Article 1 of Council Directive 91/308/EEC of 10 June 1991 on Prevention of the Use of the Financial System for the Purpose of Money Laundering, and Article 6 of the United Nations Convention against Transnational Organized Crime, which are drafted in very similar terms to Article 3 of the Vienna Convention.

12 The function and work of FATF, and the text of the *Forty Recommendations* are available on the FATF website at *http://www1.OECD.org/fatf.* FATF is the source of the three-stage description of money laundering – placement, layering and integration – referred to in the text.

13 See European Commission, *Second Commission Report to the European Parliament and the Council on the Implementation of the Money Laundering Directive* XV/1116/ 97, Rev. 2 at 9-12 and Annex 6 B; Financial Action Task Force on Money Laundering, *Review of FATF Forty Recommendations Consultation Paper, 30 May 2002,* pages 97-102; Financial Action Task Force Report on Money Laundering, *Report on Money Laundering Typologies 2001-2002,* at paragraphs 75-76 (available on the FATF web site).

14 Directive 2001/97/EC of the European Parliament and the Council of 4 December 2001 Amending Council Directive 91/308/EEC on Prevention of the Use of the Financial System for the Purpose of Money Laundering.

15 The Wolfsberg AML Principles are available online at *http://www.wolfsberg-principles.com.* The Wolfsberg Group consists of the following banks: ABN Amro NV, Banco Santander Central Hispano S.A., Bank of Tokyo-Mitsubishi, Ltd, Barclays Bank; Citigroup, Credit Suisse Group, Deutsche Bank AG, Goldman Sachs; HSBC, J.P. Morgan Chase, Société Générale and UBS AG.

16 See Articles 6 and 7 of the United Nations Convention against Transnational Organized Crime, adopted by resolution A/RES/55/25 of 15 November 2000 at the fifty-fifth session of the General Assembly of the United Nations; available at *http:// www.uncjin.org.*

17 Sections 327-340 of the Proceeds of Crimes Act 2002, available at *http:// www.hmso.gov.uk.*

18 Uniting and Strengthening America by Providing Appropriate Tools Required to Intercept and Obstruct Terrorism (USA Patriot Act) Act of 2001, Title III.

19 See *Sharing of Financial Records Between Jurisdictions in Connection with the Fight Against Terrorist Financing,* Basel Committee Publication No. 89, April 2002. The Basel Committee's members are Belgium, Canada, France, Germany, Italy, Japan, Luxembourg, the Netherlands, Spain, Sweden, Switzerland, the United Kingdom and the United States. It is based in the Bank of International Settlements in Basel. It has about thirty technical working groups and task forces which also meet regularly. It "formulates broad supervisory standards and guidelines and recommends statements of best practice in the expectation that individual authorities will take

steps to implement them through detailed arrangements – statutory or otherwise – which are best suited to their own national systems": see *http://www.bis.org/bcbs/aboutbcbs.htm.*

20 See Article 8.1 and 8.2 of the OECD Bribery Convention; see also Article III.10 of the Inter-American Convention against Corruption, and Article 4 of the *ICC Rules of Conduct: Extortion and Bribery in International Business Transactions* in François Vincke, Fritz Heimann & Ron Katz, *Fighting Bribery: A corporate practices manual* (ICC publication 610). [see also *Fighting Corruption: A corporate practices manual* (ICC publication 652)]

21 *Regulation (EC) No. 1606/2002 of the European Parliament and the Council of 19 July 2002 on the Application of International Accounting Standards; Official Journal* L243, 11/09/2002 P. 0001-0004.

22 The World Bank Group, *World Development Report 2002—Building Institutions for Markets,* pages 105-110; available at: *http://econ.worldbank.org/wdr/WDR2002.*

23 See, for example, Article 34(2)(b) of the *UNCITRAL Model Law;* Article 1504 of the *New Code of Civil Procedure* (France); Article 190.2.e of the Private International Law Statute (Switzerland).

24 Article V.2.b of the *New York Convention* provides:

"2. Recognition and enforcement of an arbitral award may also be refused if the competent authority in the country where recognition and enforcement is sought finds that: ......

b) The recognition or enforcement of the award would be contrary to the public policy of that country...."

25 See J. Giles Wetter, "Issues of Corruption Before International Arbitral Tribunal: the Authentic Text and True Meaning of Judge Gunnar Lagergren's 1963 Award in ICC Case No.1110," (1994) 10 *Arbitration International* 277-294.

26 For the statement of the *Westacre* arbitral tribunal, see footnote 1 above; *cf.* ICC Award 6497 of 1994, *(1999) Yearbook of Commercial Arbitration XXIV,* 71-79 at 73: "... The demonstration of the bribery nature of the agreement has to be made by the Party alleging the existence of bribes... A civil court, and in particular an arbitral tribunal, has not the power to make an official inquiry and has not the duty to search independently the truth...."

27 Judge Lagergren invoked the administration of justice as a ground to justify his approach: see J. Giles Wetter, "Issues of Corruption Before International Arbitral Tribunal: The Authentic Text and True Meaning of Judge Gunnar Lagergren's 1963 Award in ICC Case No.1110," (1994) 10 *Arbitration International,* 277-294 at 291. On the increasing public responsibilities of international commercial arbitration and the public credibility challenge facing modern arbitrators, a phenomenon particularly associated with the growth of investor-State arbitrations, see Bernardo M. Cremades and David J. A. Cairns, "The Brave New World of Global Arbitration," *(2002) 3 Journal of World Investment,* 173-209, at 192-209.

28 The World Bank Group, *World Development Report 2002 – Building Institutions for Markets*, page 106, available at: *http://econ.worldbank.org/wdr/WDR2002*.

29 The US Department of Justice web site on the *Foreign Corrupt Practices Act* refer to these "red flags": "... unusual payment patterns or financial arrangements, a history of corruption in the country, a refusal by the foreign joint venture partner or representative to provide a certification that it will not take any action in furtherance of an unlawful offer, promise, or payment to a foreign public official and not take any act that would cause the U.S. firm to be in violation of the FCPA, unusually high commissions, lack of transparency in expenses and accounting records, apparent lack of qualifications or resources on the part of the joint venture partner or representative to perform the services offered, and whether the joint venture partner or representative has been recommended by an official of the potential governmental customer...":

See *http://www.usdoj.gov/criminal/fraud/fcpa/dojdocb.htm*. *See also* François Vincke, Fritz Heimann & Ron Katz *Fighting Bribery: A corporate practices manual* (ICC publication 610), Chapter 4 (The Role of Agents and Sales Representatives). [see also *Fighting Corruption: A corporate practices manual* (ICC publication 652)]. Matthias Scherer "Circumstantial Evidence in Corruption Cases before International Arbitral Tribunals" [2002] *Int. A.L.R.* 29-40; Karen Mills "Corruption and Other Illegality in the Formation and Performance of Contracts and in the Conduct of Arbitration Relating Thereto" *[2002] Int. A.L.R. 126-132;* and the evaluation of "an accumulation of indications" by the Paris Court of Appeal in *European Gas Turbines SA v. Westman International Limited (1995) Yearbook of Commercial Arbitration XX 198-207.*

30 Article 8.1 of the *OECD Bribery Convention*.

31 See, for example, François Vincke, Fritz Heimann & Ron Katz, *Fighting Bribery: A corporate practices manual* (ICC publication 610) Chapter 6 (Money Laundering). [see also *Fighting Corruption: A corporate practices manual* (ICC publication 652)].

32 See Kristine Karsten, "Money Laundering: How It Works and Why You Should be Concerned," Paper presented to the ICC Institute of World Business Law, 22 Annual Meeting, November 2002, (p. 15 of this book)

33 Article 30 of the UNCITRAL Model Law provides that an award by consent can be made "...if requested by the parties and not objected to by the arbitral tribunal...." During the drafting of the Model Law, concerns were expressed regarding parties seeking awards by consent in cases involving fraud, competition and income tax law violations and conspiracy, and the proposal that an arbitral tribunal should have no discretion to refuse an award recording agreed settlement terms was rejected: see Howard H. Hotlzmann and Joseph E. Neuhaus, *A Guide to the UNCITRAL Model Law On International Commercial Arbitration: Legislative History and Commentary* (T.M.C. Asser Institut, The Hague, 1989) at 822-835. On the Iran-United States Claims Tribunal, see Stewart Abercrombie Baker and Mark David Davis, *The Uncitral Arbitration Rules in Practice: The Experience of the Iran-United States Claims Tribunal* (Kluwers, 1992), 184-189.

34 Ahmed S. El Kosheri and Philippe Leboulanger, L'arbitrage face à la corruption et aux trafics d'influence, *(1984) 3 Revue de l'Arbitrage 3-18*. See also the observations on this issue at J. Giles Wetter, "Issues of Corruption Before International Arbitral Tribunal: The Authentic Text and True Meaning of Judge Gunnar Lagergren's 1963 Award in ICC Case No.1110," (1994) 10 *Arbitration International*, 277-294 at 278-279.

35 A number of recent articles have explored the difficult issue of proof of corruption in international arbitration; see, for example, Matthias Scherer, "Circumstantial Evidence in Corruption Cases Before International Arbitral Tribunals," *[2002] Int. A.L.R. 29-40*; José Rosell and Harvey Prager, "Illicit Commissions and International Arbitration," *[1999] 15 Arbitration International 329-348*.

36 ICC Award 6497 of 1994, (*1999) Yearbook of Commercial Arbitration XXIV 71-79*, at 73.

37 "...The enterprise having benefited from the bribes (i.e., having obtained substantial contracts thanks to the bribes) has not a better moral position than the enterprise having organised the payment of the bribes. The nullity of the agreement is generally only beneficial to the former, and thus possibly inequitable. But this is legally irrelevant.": ICC Award 6497 of 1994, (*1999) Yearbook of Commercial Arbitration XXIV 71-79*, at 72.

6

The role of the expert in arbitration

By Arthur Harverd
Chartered Accountant;
Past Chairman, The Chartered Institute of Arbitrators,
London, United Kingdom

INTRODUCTION

In this paper the role of the expert in dealing with issues of money laundering, corruption and fraud in arbitration is examined. Given the nature of these activities the expert is likely to be a qualified professional accountant, although other relevant professional experience may be equally valid, e.g. banking. The expert's role is considered from three perspectives, namely that as an expert appointed to assist one or (jointly) all of the parties, as expert appointed to the arbitral tribunal and, third, the expert as a member of the arbitral tribunal participating in the determination of the dispute.

In view of recent well-known accounting scandals I will first examine the subjective nature of financial statements, which impacts significantly on issues of financial wrongdoing, and consider how the concept of materiality can weaken the boundaries between acceptable commercial behaviour and fraud. Examples of accounts manipulation with particular reference to recent wellpublicised allegations will be explored. The move to tighten accounting standards and regulation generally in light of recent difficulties will be explained.

Finally, examples of transactions which may indicate that money laundering, corruption or fraud has taken place are given together with a brief note on the relationship between the expert and law enforcement authorities.

1. THE SUBJECTIVE NATURE OF FINANCIAL STATEMENTS

It may be thought that the treatment of accounting transactions in financial statements is fairly straightforward because accounting transactions are seemingly simple matters of fact. Money is earned and spent, profits are taxed, funds are invested or borrowed. But financial statements are not necessarily limited to matters of fact. There is scope for the use of subjective assessment adequately to reflect the nature of the transaction. Most such assessments are entirely legitimate, but where they go beyond what is properly reasonable they may stray into the area of wrongdoing. Expert opinion may then be needed to provide an informed view as to whether the treatment is reasonable and appropriate or is wrong.

The simplest way of demonstrating the subjective nature of financial statements is to draw attention to my brand new Chester Barrie Savile Row suit that I am wearing for the first time today. For the purposes of this illustration it will be assumed that the tax authorities have agreed that the purchase of the suit is permitted for business purposes and may be shown in business accounts. A Chester Barrie suit is made to the highest tailoring standards, even though it is ready made, and compares favourably to an expensive suit hand-made in Savile Row. Until recently Chester Barrie suits sold for about £800 in selected menswear shops. A few months ago the Chester Barrie company went into liquidation.

An enterprising retailer purchased bulk quantities of stock from the liquidator and advertised Chester Barrie suits at a sale price of £265. For the discerning male consumer this was an unbelievable bargain. I visited the store immediately and discovered that if you purchased two suits the price was further reduced to £250 per suit. I bought two and could hardly believe my good fortune. On returning to my car with my new possessions, my pleasure was somewhat dampened to discover a parking ticket on the windscreen. In my anticipation of a bargain I had not noticed the parking restriction. I was fined £30.

This leads to a number of important accounting issues. First, if I write off the cost of each suit as an expense in the profit and loss account in the current year, has each suit cost me £250 or has it cost £265, i.e. the basic £250 plus £15, being half of the cost of the £30 parking fine which I would not have incurred had I not gone shopping?

But the bigger issue is that the suits, being of a high quality, will last for many years. As such, they constitute an asset which can be recorded in the balance sheet. Each year a proportion of their value can be expensed in the profit and loss account as depreciation or amortisation, representing the value that I have obtained from the suits by wearing them in each period. The remaining value of the suits, after depreciation, will continue to be carried in the balance sheet as an asset.

What is the appropriate value of the suits that should be recorded in the balance sheet? At one level the initial value of each suit can either be £250 or £265, depending on how I treat the parking fine. But they are really £800 suits; I just happened to get them at bargain prices. The real value of each is £800, so £1,600 can be shown initially in the balance sheet as the value of the asset. However, as the manufacturer is in liquidation the suits are no longer available to be purchased for £800. An equivalent suit would need to be hand-made by a Savile Row tailor. This would cost at least £1,500 per suit which is the replacement cost. The subjective nature of value means that I can record the value of each suit in my balance sheet at any one of four values, £250, £265, £800 or the replacement cost of £1,500.

The value in the balance sheet will help to establish the amount of the annual depreciation charge, the higher the asset value, the more being available to be written off as a depreciation expense each year. But this raises another problem. Over how many years should the suits be depreciated? Is it three years, five years, eight years, or are you one of those who takes such good care of clothes that the suits will last in good condition for fifteen years or more? So there is a further subjective assessment to be made regarding the number of years that the suits will be depreciated.

Next, there is the method of depreciation. Should the suits be depreciated by the same amount each year, or do you take into account what happens in practice? Suits looks fresher and sharper in their first year or two of use, however well maintained they are, compared to subsequent years. So depreciation can be accelerated in the first two years to reflect this fact, writing off, say, two-thirds of the value and thereafter depreciating the balance on an equal basis for however many years you want to write it off.

It is thus evident that a simple financial transaction, namely the purchase of a heavily discounted suit at a cost of £250, or is it really £265, can be reflected in the financial statements in many different ways. If this extent of subjectivity and variation can be introduced into this transaction it will be recognised that in the world of complex commercial activities, the range of alternative accounting treatments that can be introduced to reflect business transactions is almost infinite. Expert opinion is needed to assess what is, and what is not, a reasonable and valid treatment in the circumstances of the case.

Subjectivity in accounting treatment can be further complicated by the concept of materiality. Take the £15 parking fine per suit. It is not a vast sum and it may easily be considered to represent part of the cost of the suit. But if the fine was much larger, which it might have been had I not settled payment quickly, the extra amount could be material to the cost of the suits and it could be necessary to ask whether it was appropriate that the fine be added to the capitalised value of the suits in the balance sheet instead of being expensed in the year in which it was incurred.

2.   OPPORTUNITIES FOR MANIPULATING ACCOUNTS

With this understanding of how subjective assessments can affect the treatment of accounting transactions, we can examine some typical areas where financial transactions may be wrongfully manipulated. A few examples are:

Revenue
- Advancing or delaying the recognition of sales
- Manipulating rebates and discounts
- Under or over providing for bad debts

Expenses
- Under or over accruals
- Delaying or advancing expenses
- Manipulating rebates and discounts
- Misrecording capital or revenue items

Inventory
- False quality
- False quantity
- False valuation

Cash

- Hidden pledges relating to cash deposits

Other

- Manipulating transfer prices
- Misuse of inter-company and suspense accounts

3.   CURRENT ACCOUNTING SCANDALS

With this understanding of how financial statements can be manipulated we can examine some of the recent accounting scandals that have rocked corporate America. In one case it is suggested that a corporation has concealed rising expenditure that would otherwise have depleted profits and threatened the share price of the company. Expenditure was apparently capitalised and carried forward in the balance sheet as an asset, rather than being written off as an expense in the year in which it was incurred. It has been reported, for example, that the cost of plane flights to inspect possible new sites for the company's expanding telecommunications network was treated as capital expenditure. For the financial year 2001 and the first quarter of 2002 some US $3.8 billion of operating costs were said to have been treated as capital expenditure. Without these transfers, the corporation would have made losses during these periods instead of profit of US $1.4 billion in 2001 and US $130 million in the first quarter of 2002.

Treating some employee costs as capital expenditure is deemed legitimate by many telecommunications operators, as the expenditure is considered to represent capital investment for future profit depending on the nature of the work of the employees. The key difference with one corporation under scrutiny was said to be the scale of the capitalisation, i.e. it was an issue of materiality. Newspaper reports suggest that the US $3.8 billion which was capitalised represented 39% of the corporation's total capital expenditure for the periods indicated, which compare to about 15% for some of its major competitors. Since the investigation commenced it has been suggested that in the years 1999 and 2000 certain reserves were reversed into income, hence the total overstatement of earnings is alleged to be at least US $7.2 billion. Furthermore, it has been reported that the corporation may write off US $50.6 billion of intangible assets when it restates its accounts for the years 2000 to 2002.

In a second case the essence of the problem was, apparently, to remove trading activities from the core of the business by putting them into separate partnerships, thereby enabling the debt and, where appropriate, profits, to be withheld from the company's financial statements. It has been reported that the US Senate Investigation Committee believes that if the company under investigation had properly accounted for certain transactions as debt, the debt load of the company would have increased by 40% and the cashflow operations would have been halved.

Organisations where fraud is uncovered often display a number of similar characteristics. These include a dominant leadership, the sidelining of the internal audit department, an intense pressure to meet the predictions of financial analysts and others, orders to forbid employees talking to the external auditors and queries as to the nature and depth of the work undertaken by the auditors. These are matters that an expert will evaluate in forming a view as to whether wrongdoing has taken place.

4.   STRENGTHENING ACCOUNTING STANDARDS AND REGULATION

The concern caused by the recent accounting scandals has led to calls for the strengthening of accounting standards and their uniform application on a worldwide basis and for improved regulation generally.

From 2005 there will be a requirement that all listed companies within the European Union must publish consolidated financial statements that conform with international accounting standards. This will affect some 9,000 EU listed companies, of which about 500 already comply with international accounting standards[1]. Major differences exist between EU and US standards, and these are presently the subject of considerable discussion amongst the accounting regulators.

In October 2002 it was reported in the Financial Times that international and US accounting standards look set to achieve significant harmonisation as a result of an agreement reached between the International Accounting Standards Board and the US Financial Accounting Standards Board. The two Boards issued a memorandum of understanding that locks the two bodies into a long-term collaboration project on convergence.

The project is expected to remedy deficiencies in US accounting standards exposed by recent corporate scandals, and it is likely that there will be a change in the United States from a rules based to a principles based approach. The memorandum states that the two Boards are committed to the development of high-quality, compatible accounting standards that can be used for both domestic and cross-border financial reporting. They agreed to select the better standards from their two rule books in a number of areas.

The adoption of international accounting and auditing standards does not necessarily enhance the quality of financial reporting unless it is accompanied by measures to ensure the enforcement of their application. In an attempt to crack down on fraud, for example, the Finance Minister of Germany recently established a new financial taskforce to combat balance-sheet manipulation by corrupt managers and auditors. His measures include an accounting taskforce empowered to conduct snap audits at companies suspected of manipulating financial information. The US Sarbanes-Oxley Act, which was enacted in July 2002, grants considerable discretion to the SEC to execute tighter corporate supervision and includes a measure that executives may face prison sentences if they mislead their company auditors. The UK arm of one of the major big four accounting firms has stated that it intends to improve fraud detection measures in its routine audit work, and this will include the use of greater forensic skills in its testing work and checking the past track records of members of management. John Plender[2] has noted that the big four international accounting networks do not themselves guarantee common standards of quality. He pointed out that the networks located throughout the world do not operate under common ownership and are not consistently regulated or licensed. In many parts of the world the right to carry out a statutory audit is given only to local firms in which locally qualified professionals have a majority stake and management control. A World Bank/OECD report[3] stated that in practice the standards of audit performance across the networks are a voluntary matter and that lack of transparency about internal arrangements and performance standards means that buyers of the service cannot make an informed judgement. The report stated that some networks use different standards for local work and transnational work. Mr Plender noted that the networks themselves can be highly fluid in management terms in that the membership of a particular network can change relatively frequently. Hence the expert should not necessarily accept without examination the adequacy of a clean audit report signed off by a regional office of a major accounting firm.

5.   MONEY LAUNDERING

Where the possibility of money laundering arises the expert will look for some of the following typical indications, which do not attempt to be exhaustive:

- Unusually large cash deposits given the nature of the business
- Large numbers of accounts in relation to the type of business
- Transfers to financial centres known for financial secrecy laws
- Frequent overrides of internal controls or policies
- Transactions incompatible with client/customer size or normal operation
- Payments by third parties
- Payments from unusual or suspicious sources

6.   CORRUPTION

Matthias Scherer[4] has noted that there is no universal definition of corruption. He has stated that from the point of view of international arbitration, it is generally accepted that giving a public official money or other advantages to favour the offering party or his or her principal is incompatible with public policy, whatever the applicable law. Mr Scherer examined the type of circum-stantial evidence often found to surround the possibility of corruption. These include vague contractual terms which may hide the illegal intentions of the parties. The conduct of the parties is, however, usually a more trust-worthy guide than the terms of the contract. While parties will be aware that documents may be created to hide their true intentions, documentary evidence from the time before the dispute arose between the parties often bears out their common understanding of the contract. Such documents may provide invaluable evidence. A party's refusal to allow the arbitral tribunal access to such documents may lead the tribunal to draw an adverse inference[5].

An unusually high commission may suggest corrupt practices, but the amount of the commission must be examined in perspective; whether a fee is unusually high can only be established in the light of all the circumstances. The fact that levels of corruption are high in certain countries does not necessarily constitute evidence of corruption in a particular case.

In considering whether corrupt practices have taken place, the expert will want to examine all relevant records, and a refusal to provide such records may be considered decisive circumstantial evidence for the irregularity of the payments. In an ICC arbitration, where the agent refused to disclose information about its group structure, the arbitral tribunal concluded that this was a case of corruption[6].

It will often be the expert who undertakes the investigation into allegations of corrupt practices, and he should be able to assist in identifying and classifying the transactions which are the subject of the allegations.

7.   PERJURY

Perjury is an issue that often arises in arbitration, as it does in litigation. Michael Watson[7] has noted the prevalence of this practice and quoted an eminent American legal commentator who once estimated that perjury was committed in 50% of all contested civil cases, in 75% of all criminal cases, and in 90% of all divorce cases. Watson explained that there are two elements to perjury, a "wilful" statement by a witness which "he knows to be false or does not know to be true". The motive is irrelevant. It has been held that a witness who gives evidence which is literally true but is intended to give a false impression commits perjury. In one case a witness put a mouse in the mouth of a dead testator, then swore that "there was life in" his body. He was duly convicted of perjury[8].

It will be for the expert to expose perjury by the deployment of better evidence and the demonstration of inconsistency on the part of the perjurer.

8.   THE ROLE OF THE EXPERT: GENERAL MATTERS

Some party-appointed experts have been criticised for the degree of partisanship that they have shown in presenting their opinions. This smacks more of advocacy than the expression of independent and objective expert opinion. As part of the Woolf reforms of court procedures introduced in England a few years ago, the new Civil Procedure Rules ("the CPR") now contain, as Part 35, a section dealing with experts and assessors. It is the duty of an expert to help the court on the matters within his expertise, and this duty overrides any obligation to the person from whom he has received instructions or by whom he is paid. The Rules specify the form and content of experts' reports which are addressed to the court. Expert reports presented to English arbitral tribunals adopt the same approach, and the Rules state as follows:

An expert's report should be addressed to the court and not to the party from whom the expert has received his instructions.

An expert's report must:

1. Give details of the expert's qualifications.

2. Give details of any literature or other material which the expert has relied on in making the report.

3. Say who carried out any test or experiment which the expert has used for the report and whether or not the test or experiment has been carried out under the expert's supervision.

4. Give the qualifications of the person who carried out any such test or experiment, and

5. where there is a range of opinion on the matters dealt with in the report:
   i.   summarise the range of opinion, and
   ii. give reasons for his own opinion.

6. Contain a summary of the conclusions reached.

7. Contain a statement that the expert understands his duty to the court and has complied with that duty, and

8. contain a statement setting out the substance of all material instructions (whether written or oral). The statement should summarise the facts and instructions given to the expert which are material to the opinions expressed in the report or upon which those opinions are based.

An expert's report must be verified by a statement of truth as well as containing the statements required in paragraphs 7 and 8 above.

The form of the statement of truth is as follows:
"I believe that the facts I have stated in this report are true and that the opinions I have expressed are correct."

Following the introduction of the CPR Rules, the Commercial Court in London issued guidance notes in respect of expert evidence given in cases before it. These are as follows:

1. It is the duty of an expert to help the court on the matters within his expertise. This duty is paramount and overrides any obligation to the person from whom the expert has received instructions or by whom he is paid.

2. Expert evidence presented to the court should be, and should be seen to be, the independent product of the expert uninfluenced by the exigencies of litigation.

3. An expert witness should provide independent assistance to the court by way of objective unbiased opinion in relation to matters within his expertise. An expert witness should never assume the role of an advocate.

4. An expert witness should not omit to consider material facts which could detract from his concluded opinion.

5. An expert witness should make it clear when a particular question or issue falls outside his expertise.

6. If an expert's opinion is not properly researched because he considers that insufficient data is available, then this must be stated with an indication that the opinion is no more than a provisional one.

7. In a case where an expert witness who has prepared a report could not assert that the report contained the truth, the whole truth and nothing but the truth without some qualification, that qualification should be stated in the report.

8. If, after exchange of reports, an expert witness changes his view on a material matter having read another expert's report or for any other reason, such change of view should be communicated in writing (through legal representatives) to the other side without delay, and when appropriate to the court.

Until publication of the CPR the duties of the expert had been summarised in a 1993 case *The Ikarian Reefer*[9]. The principles set out in this case need to be extended in accordance with the CPR and an updated restatement of *The Ikarian Reefer* principles have been included in *Anglo Group Plc v Winther Brown & Co Ltd*[10], which is a recent 2000 case. The judgement included the following:

1. An expert witness should at all stages in the procedure, on the basis of the evidence as he understands it, provide independent assistance to the court and the parties by way of objective unbiased opinion in relation to matters within his expertise. This applies as much to the initial meetings of experts as to evidence at trial. An expert witness should never assume the role of an advocate.

2. The expert's evidence should normally be confined to technical matters on which the court will be assisted by receiving an explanation, or to evidence of

common professional practice. The expert witness should not give evidence or opinions as to what the expert himself would have done in similar circumstances or otherwise seek to usurp the role of the judge.

3. He should co-operate with the expert of the other party or parties in attempting to narrow the technical issues in dispute at the earliest possible stage of the procedure and to eliminate or place in context any peripheral issues. He should co-operate with the other expert(s) in attending without prejudice meetings as necessary and in seeking to find areas of agreement and to define precisely areas of disagreement to be set out in the joint statement of experts ordered by the court.

4. The expert evidence presented to the court should be, and be seen to be, the independent product of the expert uninfluenced as to form or content by the exigencies of the litigation.

5. An expert witness should state the facts or assumptions upon which his opinion is based. He should not omit to consider material facts which could detract from his concluded opinion.

6. An expert witness should make it clear when a particular question or issue falls outside his expertise.

7. Where an expert is of the opinion that his conclusions are based on inadequate factual information he should say so explicitly.

The above Rules and principles clarify the role and duties of experts in court in England and Wales and, by implication, in arbitral proceedings. In *Edwin John Stevens v R J Gullis and David Pile*[11] the Court of Appeal held that an expert witness was barred from giving evidence because he had failed to comply with the CPR requirements for experts; in particular, his report did not contain a statement that he understood his duty to the court and that he had complied with that duty, and his report did not contain a statement setting out the substance of all material instructions (whether written or oral).

The new Rules and guidelines will undoubtedly improve the objectivity of expert reports and help to ensure that experts examine and report on all of the issues in the round rather than focussing narrowly on their clients' position. In the accounting field they should reduce, for example, the type of conflicting expert reports produced in loss of profit claims where one expert produces an unreasonably high figure and the other expert produces an equally unrealistic low figure. This type of report is a clear example of advocacy on the part of the expert.

9.   THE ROLE OF THE EXPERT APPOINTED BY A PARTY

The new requirements for experts do not entirely eliminate the problem of advocacy, for it seems to me that one form of what might be termed advocacy is permissible when giving accounting evidence. This arises when a particular accounting transaction may be treated in a subjective manner. While the duty of the expert is to examine all possible treatments of the particular transaction, the expert may be able legitimately to advance the treatment that is most convenient for his instructing party's case if he can demonstrate that the treat-ment is permissible in the circumstances of the case, even if the treatment may be unusual. It would then be for the arbitral tribunal to determine whether the treatment was appropriate in the particular case or whether it provided evidence of wrongdoing by the party.

The new CPR do not deal fully with one problem which especially affects accountant experts. Because of its detailed nature, much of an accountant's work is traditionally delegated to junior staff. Thus, for example, junior audit staff undertake work on an audit assignment and bring technical problems to the attention of more senior staff as they arise. These difficulties will be cleared at increasingly senior levels, leaving only the most complex issues for the partner to resolve. When acting as an expert witness before a court or an arbitral tribunal, routine delegation of this nature is far from satisfactory, as the expert accountant will not have a sufficient grasp of the detail to withstand close cross-examination at the trial. There is no difficulty in delegating tranches of work in a forensic exercise, and the CPR allow for this, as noted above, but the expert accountant will need to be very precise as to the nature of the work that is delegated and what he expects to achieve as a result of that delegation. In order to delegate work effectively, the expert must have full command of his brief.

There is no substitute for the expert doing much of the detailed work himself, partly because in doing so he may identify matters that may be of critical importance in the dispute that may otherwise be missed by less-experienced junior staff. Identifying new issues in a case is an important part of the expert accountant's duties. This can lead to him suggesting amendments to his terms of reference which can play a crucial role in the outcome of the proceedings.

10. ROLE OF THE TRIBUNAL-APPOINTED EXPERT

A tribunal-appointed expert, or one appointed jointly by the parties, is independent of the parties. He will be able to present his opinions objectively without any advocacy. As a tribunal-appointed expert he may, of course, be questioned by the parties as to the appropriateness of his opinions and he will need to demonstrate that he has carefully thought through all of the implications of the views that he has expressed.

A tribunal-appointed expert can fulfil one other important function. He can undertake confidential investigative work where so instructed into accounting and other records that are not otherwise subject to disclosure in order to identify disclosable information that may be buried in material to which one of the parties has no entitlement to access. The tribunal-appointed expert will be able to examine this material, having signed a confidentiality agreement, and report to the tribunal and the parties on the information which he has extracted from the records and which are relevant to the dispute. He will be available for examination by the parties on the information that he presents and the opinions that he expresses thereon.

11. THE EXPERT AS A MEMBER OF THE TRIBUNAL

In some jurisdictions and in many international arbitrations, experts in particular fields are regularly appointed as sole arbitrator or as a member of a three- person arbitral tribunal. They are able to bring to bear their considerable experience of technical fields such as engineering, accountancy, shipping and construction to an evaluation of the technical issues that are in dispute. As arbitrator, the expert is likely to seek a high standard of presentation of the issues by the party-appointed experts and may, after the advocates have completed their oral examination of the experts, ask more penetrating questions than can be put by the non-technical expert advocates. The answers to these additional questions may yield the responses that are decisive to the resolution of the technical issues that are in dispute.

12. RELATIONSHIP OF THE EXPERT WITH LAW ENFORCEMENT AUTHORITIES

The expert will need to comply with his professional body in respect of the disclosure or reporting of fraudulent activities. For example, the Institute of Chartered Accountants in England and Wales has issued guidance notes for chartered accountants in respect of money laundering. It is a requirement to report any knowledge or suspicion of money laundering which relates to drug trafficking or terrorist activity.

I know of one instance where arbitrators were required to disclose confidential information to a regulatory or prosecuting authority or to the police where, during the conduct of the arbitral proceedings, the arbitrator had reason to believe that a serious crime may have been involved or that a serious breach of the regulatory rules had been committed or that he was under a legal duty to disclose the information and the disclosure was made in good faith to the appropriate authority. This requirement appeared in the 1992 edition of The Chartered Institute of Arbitrators Consumer Arbitration Scheme for the Finance Intermediaries, Managers and Brokers Regulatory Association (FIMBRA). This scheme was terminated following the demise of FIMBRA as a result of a merger with the UK Personal Investment Authority in the mid-1990's.

.

FOOTNOTES

1 D. Cairns, "International standards and the switch to IAS in 2005." Paper presented at a conference on fraud organised in London by The Institute of Chartered Accountants in England and Wales, September 2002.

2 J. Plender, Financial Times, London, 26 June 2002.

3 "Regulatory reform and trade liberalisation in services: the benefits and limitations of strengthening GATS rules". Accountancy Services, OECD-World Bank, March 2002.

4 M. Scherer, "Circumstantial evidence in corruption cases before international arbitral tribunals", International Arbitration Law Review, London, Sweet & Maxwell Ltd, Vol 5, Issue 2, May 2002.

5 IBA Rules on the Taking of Evidence in International Commercial Arbitration, Arts 9.4 and 9.5.

6 ICC Case No. 3916 (1982), Collection of ICC Arbitral Awards 1974-85, S507, 510.

7 Dr Michael Watson, Bath Spa University College, UK. "The Prevalence of Perjury", a paper awaiting publication in a journal for magistrates.

8 Disney's Criminal Law, (second edition, 1923), 128.

9 National Justice Compania Naviera SA v Prudential Assurance Co. The Ikerian Reefer. [1993] 2 Lloyd's Rep. 68.

10 Anglo Group Plc v Winther Brown & Co Ltd and Others, [2000]; LTL 21/3/2000; (2000) 1T + CLR 559 (2000) 72 Con LR 118.

11 Edwin John Stevens v R J Gullis and David Pile [1999]; LTL 27/9/99, Extempore, TLR 6/10/99; ILR 14/10/99; (1999) CILL 1546; (1999) BLR 394; (2000) 1 All ER 527; (2001) 73, Con LR 42.

7

Arbitration case law on bribery:
Issues of arbitrability, contract validity, merits and evidence

By Antonio Crivellaro
Professor of International Trade Law, Padua University, Italy;
Partner, Bonelli Erede Pappalardo, Milan, Italy;
Council Member, ICC Institute of World Business Law

1. THE AGREEMENT GIVING RISE TO THE DISPUTE

a) "Agency" agreements

Under such agreements, a principal confers on an agent the task of assisting the principal in obtaining the award of a (main) contract, usually a construction, engineering, supply, erection or turn-key contract, called for tender by an employer or owner (in general a State entity or public agency) in a given importing country.

Although such an agreement contemplates – in substance – the use of an intermediary, international practice refrains from using the word *intermediation* when defining the relationship. The parties refer to it, instead, as an agency or consultancy relationship or call their agreement an assistance agreement or sponsorship or brokerage agreement, or the like.

The reason why reference to an intermediary is avoided is twofold. First, recourse to an intermediary in the award of a public works contract can be prohibited, and sometimes severely sanctioned, by the procurement laws of the importing country. Second, the parties are unwilling to disclose the genuine object and nature of their agreement and tend to present it as a different or ordinary commercial operation.

International practice shows a great degree of uniformity in the agreements here at issue.

Notwithstanding the many names they go under, all such agreements are entered into in writing, an indication that both parties intend to define their reciprocal rights and obligations through an instrument capable of being formally enforced in case of dispute. Moreover, the contents and structure of the clauses are drawn up according to standard forms.

b) The kinds of services assigned to the agent

The agent undertakes to render certain services in view of obtaining the award of one or more main contracts to the principal in the importing country. The services which are formally indicated in the agreement may include market research, assistance in the preparation of the offer, organization of meetings, supply of information concerning the tendered project, consultancy as to local legislation or regulations in areas affecting the cost of the tendered project, investigations of a technical, or contractual or economic nature and whatever other kinds of assistance may be deemed necessary to enhance the principal's likelihood of winning the tender.

Irrespective of the list or number of services assigned to the agent, the agreement contains a clause expressly linking the services to their underlying purpose, that is, the award of the main contract to the principal.

The language of the relevant clauses may in some occasions reveal that, in addition to the services overtly assigned to the agent by the express terms of the agreement, other and more substantive or fundamental services are undertaken by him, implicitly. Such services, in short, consist of a *trafic d'influence* to be exerted in the interest of the principal.

The express and implied terms correspond more closely and transparently if, in the importing country, an agency relationship is permitted when the bidder is a foreign contractor or are even made mandatory by local procurement laws (e.g., the Gulf area).

Frequently, the nature of the agent – in general an offshore company having no corporate structure – is in apparent contradiction with the quantity or types of services listed in the agreement, which may include costly investi-gations impossible to perform without an appropriate organization and that are normally performed by the principal himself. In such cases, the long list of nominal services serves the purpose of justifying the amount of the agent's remuneration, more than that of establishing the true performance obligations to be satisfied by the agent.

c)   Remuneration of the agent

The agent is remunerated through a percentage fee applied to the value of the main contract awarded to the principal. As a rule, payment of the agent's fee is strictly contingent on the award of the main contract to the principal. The agreement typically states clearly that no payment is due to the agent if there is no award, not even reimbursement of costs. In other words, the agent assumes the risk not only of not earning his fee, but also of bearing the costs of his services if the principal is not the successful bidder.

If the main contract is awarded to the principal, the fee due to the agent is generally calculated as a pro-rata portion of the payments made to the principal by the employer under the main contract. Therefore, payment is not linked to the quality of the performance rendered by the agent or to the quantity of his services. Payment is linked exclusively to events concerning the life of the main contract, i.e., the commercial success of the trade operation. Of course, commercial success also depends on the professionalism of the agent. However, the agent could deploy his best efforts, but remain unpaid if the main contract is awarded to another bidder.

These are further confirmations that the agent is, in reality, an intermediary. Were the agent a mere service provider, such as a provider of consultancy or professional advice, he would be paid on the basis of the services actually rendered, irrespective of the commercial outcome of the main operation.

If the agent is, in reality, an intermediary, it must be logically inferred that he has been entrusted by the principal, expressly or tacitly, with procuring contacts from a third person or entity, who must be a person or entity capable of playing a role or exerting an influence in the decision concerning the award of the main contract.

d) Amount of the remuneration

The most striking feature in this kind of agency agreement is the clause establishing the *quantum* of the agent's remuneration or commission.

It normally consists of a substantial amount, out of all proportion with the content and nature of the services listed as those to be undertaken by the agent under the official terms of the agreement. No such service could *per se* justify that amount, which in practice usually corresponds to a very significant portion of the price of the main contract.

One is inevitably led to infer that this remuneration covers the interest of some other entity, which can only be an entity connected with the persons who have the power to award the main contract to a certain bidder, rather than to another.

e) Governing law clause

A further traditional feature of such agreements is that they invariably have a governing law clause that stipulates the applicable law to be the law of a third country, different from the country of performance of the main contract (unless in the country of performance of the main contract, the services of an intermediary are permitted or even required, e.g., the Gulf area).

In many cases, the foreign law chosen by the parties is Swiss law. The reason is, perhaps, that Swiss law does not prohibit the (proper) use of agents in public procurements (although corruption, of course, is punishable) or that the venue of the arbitration foreseen in the agreement is frequently Switzerland.

f) Arbitration agreement

The agreement contains a clause submitting disputes to international arbitration, the venue of which is in a third country, different from the country of performance of the main contract and from the countries of the parties.

This constant preference is probably explained by the fact that arbitrators do not have the same investigative powers as a national judge or may apply a standard of proof different from that applied by a national judge.

Principal and agent are undoubtedly aware that a national judge may be more willing to inquire *ex officio* into the nature of their agreement, whether or not the parties raise the issue either in their agreement or during the proceedings. The parties may wish to avoid such an outcome and prefer that any dispute be settled through an arbitral award which is, *inter alia,* confidential and issued at the end of confidential proceedings, whilst judicial proceedings before national courts are not protected by confidentiality.

2. HOW DISPUTES ARISE

In practice, disputes are referred to arbitration in one of the following cases:

- the agent initiates arbitration because the principal refuses to pay the commission, objecting that services were not rendered or that the agreement was illegal and invalid;

- the principal initiates arbitration in an attempt to recover a commission paid in part or in full to the agent, disputing the legality of the contract; or

- a dispute arises in connection with the main contract between the principal and the employer, whereby the employer claims that the main contract was induced by corruption or bribery and is therefore illegal.

3. PARTIES' BEHAVIOR BEFORE THE ARBITRATORS

With regard to the issue of whether the agency agreement entailed bribery, the parties' behavior falls, in general, into one of two patterns:

- The parties superficially agree that there was to be no bribery, but the principal refuses payment to the agent on other grounds, e.g., the services were not rendered by the agent, the agent was inefficient or the award of the main contract was not the result of the agent's efforts and the agent deserves no credit for it, that is, there was no cause-and-effect link between the award of the contract and the agent's intervention. As for the agent, he claims payment of the agreed fee, maintaining that his entitlement to payment derives automatically from the successful award of the main contract to the principal, to the exclusion of any other conditions.

- Alternatively, the principal denies payment to the agent, arguing that the real intent of the agency agreement was to corrupt or influence the authorities or public officials responsible for awarding the main contract, while the agent counters by arguing that no bribery has been proven and that the agreement is fully enforceable in law.

4.   ARBITRATORS' REACTION

As is clear from the awards summarized hereinafter, the arbitrators' approach varies from case to case, following one of several patterns:

(i)   they refuse to arbitrate the dispute; or

(ii)   they accept jurisdiction on the theory of severability of the arbitration agreement, but uphold *ex officio* international standards of public policy and declare the agency agreement invalid and dismiss the claim for payment submitted by the agent; or

(iii)   either on request of a party (the respondent) or *ex officio,* they find in the agency agreement itself certain "indicia" that the agency conceals a bribery case; or

(iv)   if an allegation of bribery is raised by the respondent, they require a "low standard" of proof or resort to a "presumption" in order to declare the agency agreement invalid; or

(v)   if an allegation of bribery is raised, they require a "high standard" of proof of corruption and, failing such proof, declare the agreement valid and uphold the agent's claim to payment; or

(vi)   they do not find bribery to have been established by the evidence, but dismiss the agent's claim for payment and refuse to enforce the agency agreement on the ground that the agreement is illicit under mandatory provisions of the procurement law of the importing country, prohibiting recourse to intermediaries when contracting with the State or State entities; or

(vii)   they apply the public policy rules of the national law which, by the parties' choice, governs the agreement, disregarding the equivalent public policy rules of the law of the importing country; or

(viii) they inquire whether the arbitration agreement contained in the main contract awarded to the principal has been, as such, induced by corruption and fraud.

5.   THE CASE LAW

Among the twenty-five cases collected in the attached exhibit:

(i)   In only one case was jurisdiction refused by the arbitrator (Case No. 1 of the attached collection). This is the oldest arbitral decision in this matter, known by the name of the arbitrator, Mr Lagergren. He declined jurisdiction on the basis that a dispute arising from bribery inevitably results, in his opinion, in its non-arbitrability.

(ii)   In three cases, the agreement was *ex officio* declared illegal and invalid, either because its purpose was illicit according to the law chosen by the parties to govern their agreement (Case No. 2) or because it contravened international public policy (Case No. 3) or because an award enforcing the contract would be contrary to the public policy of the country in which the award would be enforced (Case No. 5).

(iii)   In three cases, the arbitrators applied direct or indirect "indicia" showing that the agreement was illegal.

In Case No. 10, the arbitrators ruled that there was a conflict between the apparent or alleged intention and the real intention of the parties.

In Case No. 11, the arbitrators concluded that the violation by an engineering firm of the special fiduciary duty owed by it to an employer, for the purpose of accommodating the contractor's desire for undue payments, was contrary to public international policy and to *bonos mores* under Swiss law, the substantive law applicable to the agreement.

In Case No. 23, the arbitral tribunal identified and applied four "indicia" to prove illegality, namely: the inability of the agent to justify performance of his obligations, the duration of the agent's intervention, the method of remunerating the agent and the amount of the agent's remuneration as compared to the advantages obtained by the principal.

(iv)   In just one case, a "low" standard of proof was applied in order to establish the existence of corruption: see Case No. 11 (a violation of fiduciary duty contrary to public international policy and to *bonos mores* under Swiss law).

(v)   There were fourteen cases in which a "high" standard of proof was applied, i.e., more than 50% of the cases.

In Case No. 4, the arbitral tribunal ruled that "direct or even circumstantial evidence" was needed. Although the "consultancy price was very high," this element was not sufficient, alone, to prove corruption.

In Case No. 6 (Hilmarton case, first award), the arbitrator concluded that the evidence (witness statements and the amount of the commission) was not sufficient to establish "with certainty" the existence of corruption. He decided, however, that the agreement was in violation of Swiss public policy and hence invalid, since the agent was appointed in patent violation of Algerian law, forbidding intermediaries in administrative contracts.

In Case No. 12, the arbitral tribunal required clear proof that the amounts paid to the agent "were intended" to bribe officials to trade on their influence to obtain favors. No such proof was provided, so bribery and corruption were deemed not to have been present.

In Case No. 13 (the Westinghouse/President Marcos case), the arbitrators applied the standard of proof required in the three States (the Philippines, New Jersey and Pennsylvania) of the parties, that is, "clear and convincing evidence" of bribery. The U.S. Court applied, in the parallel case, a "lower" standard of proof, which permitted to the Court to conclude that the agent's commissions were intended to be paid, at least in part, to President Marcos.

In Case No. 14, the arbitral tribunal stated that "allusions not supported by evidence and based on suppositions" are not sufficient to prove corruption.

In Case No. 16, the proof that the agent was hired to influence the employer's award was deemed lacking. The Paris Appeal Court confirmed that no proof of traffic of influence had been provided.

In Case No. 17, "no direct or circumstantial evidence of bribery" was found.

In Case No. 18, several agency agreements were disputed, but "conclusive evidence" of bribery was not found to have been provided in the case of the vast majority of the agreements, notwithstanding the disproportion between the price paid to and the costs borne by the agent. A "high degree of probability of bribery" was, however, found in relation to one of the agreements, in which the commission amounted to the "extremely unusual" fee of 33.33%.

In Case No. 19, the majority of the arbitral tribunal ruled that "a mere suspicion by a member of the arbitral tribunal is entirely insufficient" to prove the presence of corruption. The clause "exonerating the agent *from proving his actual services*" was not considered a sufficient indication of an illicit intent.

In Cases Nos. 20, 21, 22, 24 and 25, the arbitrators ruled that "clear and convincing" evidence was needed in order to declare the agreement invalid because of corruption.

(vi) In only one case (Case No. 6: first award; annulled), the agency agreement was declared null and void, notwithstanding the lack of direct proof of bribery. Indeed, the Tribunal found the agreement to be contrary to the mandatory prohibitions of the law of the importing State (Algeria) and "therefore" contrary to international public and internal (Swiss) policy.

(vii) In five cases, the arbitrators applied the public policy principles of the law that the parties had selected to govern the agreement, rather than the public policy rules of the country in which the main contract would be performed.

In the second award in Case No. 6 (Hilmarton) and in Case No. 7, Swiss public policy was applied, instead of Algerian public policy, and the agency agreements were not deemed contrary to Swiss law.

In Case No. 8, the arbitrator affirmed that (translation) "the interests of State X are not so preponderant in relation to Swiss law that they should be taken into consideration and invalidate the contract."

In Case No. 9, the arbitrator stated that brokerage is not prohibited under Swiss law and that any prohibition of intermediaries under foreign public law is not mandatory for arbitrators sitting in Switzerland and applying Swiss law.

In Case No. 24, a violation of the US Foreign Corrupt Practices Act was not considered relevant insofar as Swiss public policy was not breached.

(viii) In one case (Case No. 15), the dispute arose between a contractor and an employer, and the latter objected that the arbitration agreement included in the main contract was invalid on the grounds that it had been induced by corruption and fraud. The arbitrators concluded that the arbitration clause could, as such, be invalid and not enforceable when it is proved that the clause itself was entered into solely because of corruption and fraud, irrespective of the possible invalidity (due to corruption) of the rest of the contract's clauses, which is a different matter.

6.   CONCLUSIONS

The case law shows that international arbitrators:

- accept jurisdiction;

- consider that their primary duty is owed to the parties and is to settle their dispute in accordance with the parties' agreement, and not a duty to be an "organ" of the international community entrusted with enforcing morality in trade operations;

- require clear proof of bribery before invalidating an agency agreement, notwithstanding any suspicions they may have;

- only in a minority of cases search for indicia of bribery on their own initiative; and

- only in few cases accord primacy to mandatory legal provisions prohibiting use of intermediaries in force in the State most closely linked to the trade operation in question, preferring generally to give precedence to the public policy rules established by the governing law as designated by the agreement between principal and agent.

The final jurisprudential trend summarized above – i.e., that of giving little weight to the mandatory provisions of any law of the importing country forbidding the use of intermediaries in public contracts tendering, and relying decisively instead on the law chosen by the parties – is open to criticism.

Indeed, this trend is in contradiction with Article 3, paragraph 3, of the Rome Convention, pursuant to which the parties' choice of a foreign law cannot, where all other points of attachment are to another specific country, result in a derogation from the imperative rules of law of that country, and with Article 7, paragraph 1, of the same Convention, providing that effect may be given to the imperative rules of law of a country whose law is not that chosen by the parties, but with which the contract at issue has close ties, to the extent the parties wish such rules of law to be applied to the contract in question pursuant to the law of that country.

International arbitrators should accept that, in order to establish the legality or validity of an agency agreement submitted to them, the cannot simply disregard the mandatory legal provisions of the importing country. They should not ignore the possibility that the principal and agent elected to stipulate their agreement to be subject to the law of a different country precisely because they sought to escape from the mandatory prohibitions of the importing country.

AWARDS

1. ICC case no. 1110 of 1963

ARBITRAL TRIBUNAL:

Sole arbitrator G. Lagergren (Sweden)

PARTIES:

Claimant: Agent from Argentina
Respondent: Contractor from UK

PLACE OF ARBITRATION:

Paris

LAW APPLICABLE TO MERITS:

Argentinian law

SUBJECT MATTERS:

Bribery and lack of jurisdiction of arbitrator.
Non-arbitrability of disputes arising from a contract violating *bonos mores* and international public policy.
Direct proof of bribery unnecessary.

SUMMARY OF FACTS:

The case concerns a contract under which a British company had engaged an Argentine intermediary to obtain a public works contract in Argentina, in return for which the intermediary was to receive a commission of 10% of the value of the contract. When the British company refused to pay the commission, the dispute was referred to Mr. Lagergren, as sole arbitrator.

REASONING OF THE TRIBUNAL:

Mr. Lagergren stated that it was "[…] in [his] judgement, plainly established from the evidence taken by [him] that the agreement between the parties contemplated the bribing of Argentine officials […]." In order to prove bribery, the arbitrator relied, firstly, on the true intention of the parties as determined by himself and on common knowledge, according to which "[…] during the Peron regime everyone wishing to do business in the Argentine was faced with the question of bribes […]." Referring to "[…] general principles denying arbitrators to entertain disputes of this nature rather than […] any national rules on arbitrability," he declined jurisdiction. He stated that "parties who ally themselves in an enterprise of the present nature must realize that they have forfeited any right to ask for assistance of the machinery of justice (national courts or arbitral tribunals) in settling their disputes."

AWARD:

The Claimant's claim was rejected for lack of jurisdiction.

PUBLISHED IN:

Yearbook Commercial Arbitration XXI (1996), p. 47.

2. ICC case no. 3913 of 1981

PARTIES:

Claimant: English company
Respondent: French contractor

LAW APPLICABLE TO THE MERITS:

French law

SUBJECT MATTER:

Contract whose purpose is the payment of "kickbacks" is null and void.

SUMMARY OF FACTS:

A French contractor asked a British company to assist it, for a fee, in obtaining certain contracts to be awarded by the government of an African country. The Claimant undertook to provide to the Respondent a number of services consisting of information and assistance aimed at facilitating to the extent possible the award of the contract to the Respondent. In exchange, the Respondent undertook to pay to the Claimant a fee of 8% of the amount of the contracts awarded, after deducting certain supplies and services included in the contracts.

REASONING OF THE TRIBUNAL:

According to the arbitral tribunal, the evidence (that is, certain documents produced and certain testimony of representatives of the parties or witnesses) showed that the commission stipulated to be due to the Claimant was to be used to pay what are commonly called "kickbacks." The arbitral tribunal concluded, accordingly, that the purpose of the agreement was illicit and immoral under French law. This rendered the agreement null and void and prevented the parties from asserting rights under it both as a matter of French domestic public policy and under (translation) "the concept of international public policy as recognized by most nations."

AWARD:

The claim was rejected.

PUBLISHED IN:

Bruno Oppetit, "Le paradoxe de la corruption à l'épreuve du droit du commerce international." *Journal du Droit International*, 1987, pp. 9, 11; Yves Derains, *Journal du Droit International*, 1984, p. 920 (notes concerning ICC case no. 2730).

3.   ICC case no. 3916 of 1982

ARBITRAL TRIBUNAL:

Sole arbitrator

PARTIES:

Claimant: Director of a department of the State of Iran
Respondent: Greek company

PLACE OF ARBITRATION:

Paris

LAW APPLICABLE TO THE MERITS:

French law

SUBJECT MATTER:

Contract that violates public policy and moral standards is null and void.

SUMMARY OF FACTS:

A Greek company and a director of a department of the State of Iran concluded a contract whereby the Iranian Claimant, acting on behalf of a "group," offered "its information and advice" to the Respondent to help it obtain orders from various Iranian authorities. The Respondent was obliged to pay to the Claimant a commission on all orders placed in the context of the contract, with a minimum of 2% of the amount of each agreement that was concluded. The Respondent was awarded several contracts by Iranian authorities, but the 1979 Iranian revolution put an end to the Respondent's activities in Iran. The Respondent paid the Claimant only a part of the promised commissions on the payments it received from the State of Iran.

REASONING OF THE TRIBUNAL:

The arbitral tribunal pointed out that it was (translation) "a matter of public knowledge that, for years [when the Greek company was working in Iran], corruption or at least the trafficking of influence was the rule [...] [and that it] was extremely difficult or impossible to be awarded public works contracts without recourse to these methods." After remarking on the surprising rapidity with which the Claimant was able to obtain contracts for the Respondent and underscoring that the Claimant had refused to provide any explanation of the nature of its intercession or the composition of its group, the arbitrator concluded that the Claimant's activities could only have been to exercise influence over those who decided with whom the State of Iran would contract. After applying French and Iranian law, the arbitrator made reference (translation): "to a legal principle generally recognized by civilized nations according to which agreements that are in serious violation of moral standards or international public policy are null and void or at least cannot be performed."

AWARD:

The arbitrator rejected the Claimant's claim.

PUBLISHED IN:

Journal du Droit International, 1984, p. 930 (with observations of S.J.); S. Jarvin and Y. Derains, *Recueil des sentences arbitrales de la CCI 1974-1985*, p. 507.

4. Interim and final awards in ICC case no. 4145 of 1983, 1984 and 1986

PARTIES:

Claimant: Establishment of Middle Eastern country X
Respondent: South Asian construction company

PLACE OF ARBITRATION:

Vienna

LAW APPLICABLE TO THE MERITS:

Swiss law

SUBJECT MATTERS:

Severability of arbitration clause.
No evidence of bribery.

SUMMARY OF FACTS:

A South Asian construction company, eager to be a successful bidder on a tender called by a Middle Eastern country, entered into a consultancy agreement with the Claimant, an establishment of the said country. The agreement described the services to be rendered by the Claimant as follows: "Consultant shall, in consideration of the compensation hereinafter agreed to be paid to it by Company, provide Company with such counsel, guidance liaison assistance, facilities, value engineering, complete tender studies [...] and shall, in general use its best efforts to promote and further the sale of the Projects." The Claimants alleged that the Respondent had failed to pay the entire sum owed to it under the consultancy agreement (US $50 million were paid, but US $16 million were not) and initiated an arbitration against the Respondent.

FIRST INTERIM AWARD:

In a first interim award, rendered in 1983, the arbitral tribunal decided the issue of jurisdiction. As the validity of the agreement in itself was an issue raised in the arbitration, the tribunal had to decide whether the arbitration agreement was affected by the alleged nullity of the contract. The tribunal ruled that the question of nullity of the contract, for reasons of public policy, illegality or otherwise, belongs to the merits and does not affect jurisdiction.

The validity of the arbitration clause has to be considered separately from the validity of the contract in which it is contained (severability of arbitration clause). The arbitral tribunal held that it had jurisdiction to decide the case.

SECOND INTERIM AWARD:

In a second interim award, rendered in 1984, the arbitral tribunal stated that the allegation of bribery was "not supported by direct evidence or even circumstantial evidence to be retained as convincing." It furthermore declared that "a fact can be considered as proven even by the way of circumstantial evidence. However such circumstantial evidence must lead to a very high probability." It stated that neither the language of the contract nor the Defendant's own witness mentioned or supposed any bribery. The arbitral tribunal stated further that, even though the consultancy price was very high, this was not "due to a sheer increase in the price [in the main contract], without counterpart–which would certainly have been suspect–but to a considerable increase in quantity and quality of the work offered by defendant in its first bid. Finally, the arbitrators did not "find sufficient reasons to arrive at the conclusion it was an agreement for bribery," stressing that the nullity implies that both parties agree on the immoral purpose to be achieved or on the immoral means to be used in order to achieve a certain result, which was not, according to the tribunal, the case in the matter in question.

The arbitral tribunal held that the agreement was valid under Swiss law and rejected the Respondent's motion to dismiss the claim on the ground of bribery.

FINAL AWARD:

In the final award, rendered in 1986, the arbitral tribunal dealt with quantum and ordered Respondent to pay a certain amount to the Claimant.

PUBLISHED IN:

Yearbook Commercial Arbitration XII (1987), p. 97;
Journal du Droit International, 1985, p. 985 (with a comment by Yves Derains).

5. ICC case no. 4219

SUBJECT MATTER:

Disregard of international public policy in favour of U.S. public policy

SUMMARY OF FACTS:

The Respondent, a party to a contract for the construction of a hotel in Egypt, challenged the arbitral tribunal's jurisdiction, claiming that the contract involved bribery of Egyptian officials through the payment of commissions to an intermediary.

REASONING OF THE TRIBUNAL:

The arbitral tribunal apparently dismissed or ignored any reference to international public policy and concentrated exclusively on determining whether U.S. public policy would be violated by an award on the merits and thus whether such an award would ultimately be enforceable in U.S. courts. The tribunal concluded that international contracts are scrutinized by U.S. courts with "special considerations," thus suggesting the existence of a doctrine of reluctance to enforce such contracts on public policy grounds.

UNPUBLISHED, MENTIONED BY:

Magnus Eriksson, "Arbitration and Contracts Involving Corrupt Practices: The Arbitrator's Dilemma, "American Review of International Arbitration", 1993, pp. 409.

6.   ICC case no. 5622; award of August of 1982 (annulled) and second award of April 1992 (Hilmarton matter)

ARBITRAL TRIBUNAL:

Sole arbitrator

PARTIES:

Claimant: English company, Hilmarton
Respondent: French company, OTV

PLACE OF ARBITRATION:

Geneva

LAW APPLICABLE TO THE MERITS:

Swiss law

SUBJECT MATTERS:

Whether corruption was proved or not.
Whether a violation of the Algerian law prohibiting recourse to intermediaries in public contracts also violated Swiss public policy.

SUMMARY OF FACTS:

OTV, desirous to be a successful bidder on a tender called by the Algerian authorities, entered into a protocol of agreement with Hilmarton, under which Hilmarton was to give legal and fiscal advice to OTV, thereby helping it to obtain the contract with the Algerian authorities. In exchange, OTV undertook to pay Hilmarton fees in an amount equal to 4% of the total amount of the primary contract. OTV was awarded the primary contract, but paid Hilmarton only 50% of the agreed commission.

FIRST AWARD:

The arbitrator examined two questions: whether it had been proved that kick-backs were paid and whether the violation of the Algerian law prohibiting the trafficking of influence implied a violation of international public policy or of Swiss public policy, with the effect of rendering the agreement null and void.

As regards the question of proof, the arbitrator concluded that the evidence (testimony and the amount of the commission) not sufficient to conclude with certainty the payment of kickbacks.

As regards Algerian law, the arbitrator noted that the prohibition on using intermediaries in contracts with the public authorities had almost certainly been violated and that this violation implied a violation of international public policy, as well as of moral standards contemplated in Article 20 of the Swiss *Code des Obligations*. As a result, he declared the agreement null and void and rejected the claim made by Hilmarton.

ANNULMENT:

On November 17, 1989, at the request of Hilmarton, the Court of Justice of the Canton of Geneva annulled the award, stating that in the present case the violation of a foreign law did not imply the violation of moral standards in Swiss law, particularly since no kickbacks were contemplated in the agreement nor proved in the arbitration. Further, the Court declared that the arbitral award was arbitrary, because the two parties had signed the agreement in full knowledge of the fact that Hilmarton would act in violation of Algerian law. It was thus unacceptable that OTV invoked, in its favour, a violation of Algerian law allegedly violating Swiss moral standards, when the said violation was an implicit part of the agreement right from the beginning. The Swiss Federal Tribunal approved the annulment on April 17, 1990.

SECOND AWARD:

Following the annulment of the first award, Hilmarton resumed ICC arbitration under Swiss law. The first arbitrator resigned and was replaced by another arbitrator, who rendered his award in April 1992. He reached a decision in conformity with the rulings of the Swiss tribunals and declared the litigated agreement valid. Hilmarton's claim was accepted.

ENFORCEMENT:

The first award was enforced in France, notwithstanding that it had been annulled in Switzerland. The second award was enforced not in France, but in Great Britain.

PUBLISHED IN:

Yearbook Commercial Arbitration XIX (1994), p. 105 (first award); *Revue de l'arbitrage*, 1993, p. 327 (first award); *Revista dell'Arbitrato*, 1992, p. 773 (first award, with a note by Andrea Giardina).

Revue de l'arbitrage, 1993, p. 315 (Court of Justice of the Canton de Geneva, Swiss Federal Tribunal); *Yearbook Commercial Arbitration XIX* (1994), p. 214 (Swiss Federal Tribunal); *Rivista dell'Arbitrato*, 1992, p. 735 (Court of Justice of the Canton of Geneva); *Rivista dell'Arbitrato*, 1992, p. 739 (Swiss Federal Tribunal).

Yearbook Commercial Arbitration XX (1995), p. 663 (Cour de Cassation); *Journal du Droit International*, 1996, p. 120 (Court of Appeal of Versailles); *Rivista dell'Arbitrato*, 1997, p. 391 (Court of Appeal of Versailles with a note by Andrea Giardina); *Rivista dell'Arbitrato*, 1992, p. 743 (Court of Appeal of Paris).

For references to the second award and its enforcement in England, see E. Brown, "Illegality and Public Policy – Enforcement of Arbitral Awards in England: *Hilmarton Limited v. Omnium de Traitement et de Valorisation S.A.,*" International Arbitration Law Review 2000, p. 31.

7. CCIG (Chambre de Commerce et d'Industrie de Genève) award of February 23, 1988

PARTIES:
Claimant: X (UK)
Respondent: Y (France/Algeria)

PLACE OF ARBITRATION:
Geneva

LAW APPLICABLE TO THE MERITS:
Swiss law

AWARD:
Prohibition of intermediaries under Algerian law is not mandatory for arbitrators sitting in Switzerland and applying Swiss law. Violation of such prohibition does not imply violation of Swiss law.

MENTIONED BY:
Matthias Scherer, "Circumstantial Evidence in Corruption Cases before International Arbitral Tribunals, *"International Arbitration Law Review"*, 2002, p. 29 (*A.S.A. Bulletin*, 1988, p. 136).

8. 1989 ICC case

ARBITRAL TRIBUNAL:
Sole arbitrator

PARTIES:

Claimant: English "Offshore" company
Respondent: Swiss company

PLACE OF ARBITRATION:

Geneva

LAW APPLICABLE TO THE MERITS:

Swiss law

SUBJECT MATTERS:

No proof of corruption.
No violation of Swiss law due to violation of a foreign law.

SUMMARY OF FACTS:

The Respondent replied to an international call for tenders issued by a State enterprise in Country X relating to the sale of 25,000 machines to that enterprise. Subsequent to the submission of its bid, the Respondent was contacted by the Claimant and the parties concluded a contract pursuant to which the Claimant, acting as a "consultant," had to advise and assist the Respondent by supplying to it all information available and necessary in order to facilitate the Respondent's selection as supplier. In exchange, the Claimant was entitled to a commission calculated on the total number of machines ordered. The Respondent was awarded contracts for the supply of 17,000 machines. The Respondent refused to pay the commission requested by the Claimant and the Claimant commenced arbitration.

REASONING OF THE TRIBUNAL:

The issue of corruption was raised during the proceedings, but the Respondent failed to show that the purpose of the contract with the Claimant was to obtain the sales contract by means of corruption of an official of State X or an agent of a State X body. The arbitrator stated that, in principle, he could have declared the contract null and void, but that no probative evidence of acts of corruption or of an intent to corrupt was submitted in the proceedings. The tribunal was thus obligated to declare the contract valid and not contrary to moral standards. With respect to a possible nullity of the contract under the laws of State X, which prohibit intermediaries, the arbitrator held that (translation): "it is not shown in the present case that the interests of X are so preponderant in relation to Swiss law that they must be taken into consideration and invalidate the contract. The arbitral tribunal observes, furthermore, in this regard, that the parties have not raised this argument nor requested the invalidation of the contract on this basis; it will thus consider the contract as valid notwithstanding the regulations of State X prohibiting intermediaries."

AWARD:

It is interesting to note that, notwithstanding the foregoing reasoning, the Claimant's claim was rejected on the grounds that it failed to prove that it had satisfied its obligations under the contract. In other words, the arbitrator decided that the agent did not fulfill its mandate (the services contemplated in the contract) and was thus not entitled to remuneration.

PUBLISHED IN:

A.S.A. Bulletin, 1993, p. 216.

9.   *Ad Hoc* award of 1989

PARTIES:

Claimant: Company from Panama
Respondent: Company from Switzerland

PLACE OF ARBITRATION:

Geneva

LAW APPLICABLE TO THE MERITS:

Swiss law

AWARD:

Brokerage is not prohibited under Swiss law. The prohibition of inter-mediaries under foreign public law is not mandatory for arbitrators sitting in Switzerland and applying Swiss law.

MENTIONED BY:

Matthias Scherer, "Circumstantial Evidence in Corruption Cases Before International Arbitral Tribunals," *International Arbitration Law Review*, 2002, p. 29 (*A.S.A. Bulletin*, 1991, pp. 239).

10.   ICC case no. 5943 of 1990

ARBITRAL TRIBUNAL:

Sole arbitrator

LAW APPLICABLE TO THE MERITS:

Korean law

SUBJECT MATTERS:

Conflict between stated (but fictitious) terms of an agreement and the true intention of the parties, which was to pay an intermediary for a completely different type of service.

Falsity of the declared intention renders the contract null under Korean law. Arbitral jurisdiction as not affected by the nullity of the agreement containing the arbitration clause.

SUMMARY OF FACTS:

The two parties concluded a contract, declaring their intention to establish a joint venture company having as its purpose the construction and management of a hotel. Certain payments were made by the Claimant, ostensibly as a contribution to the company's joint venture capital, but the money was in reality paid to a consultant engaged by the Claimant's parent company in order to obtain a successful armaments contract between the Claimant's parent company and country X. The hotel contract was conceived in order to create a vehicle for the payment of a commission on the acquisition of the armaments contract. The contract not having been obtained, the Claimant sought to be repaid.

AWARD:

The arbitrator found that, under a provision of the Korean Civil Code, a fictitious declaration of intention made in collusion with the other party was null and void. He therefore declared the payment provision in the agreement null and inapplicable and dismissed the Claimant's claim on the ground that the Claimant had no legal entitlement to restitution of an illicit or undue payment. Even though the Respondent introduced the notion of bribery in order to avoid reimbursement, the arbitrator did not apply international public policy principles or other international law principles condemning corruption. He simply denied the Claimant's right to reimbursement on the basis of Korean Civil Code.

PUBLISHED IN:

Journal du Droit International, 1996, p. 1014 (with comments by D. H.)

11. ICC case no. 6248 of 1990

PARTIES:

Claimant: Consultant of undisclosed nationality
Respondent: Contractor of undisclosed nationality

PLACE OF ARBITRATION:

Zurich

LAW APPLICABLE TO THE MERITS:

Swiss law

SUBJECT MATTERS:

Nullity of contract violating *bonos mores* under Swiss law.
Violation of international public policy by means of a commission agreement violating special fiduciary obligations to a third party.

SUMMARY OF FACTS:

Respondent contracted with an employer (party D) for the construction of a project. Party D also concluded a supervision and design contract with an engineering consulting firm (the engineer) to supervise Respondent's performance of the project. In the context of the project, Respondent hired the Claimant (a firm linked to the engineer), ostensibly as a "consultant" for the Respondent, but in fact for the purpose of persuading the engineer to exercise influence over the decisions of party D for Respondent's benefit and to disregard the special fiduciary duty owed by the engineer under the engineering contract between it and party D. Payments to be made to the Claimant under the cover of the "consultancy" arrangement were intended to be also of benefit to the engineer for his favours to the Respondent.

REASONING OF THE TRIBUNAL:

The Respondent provided some evidence that its contract with the Claimant was made for the purpose of obtaining illicit favours from the engineer, and the Claimant was incapable of seriously contesting it. The arbitral tribunal found the evidence sufficient to establish the truth of the allegation.

Applying Swiss law, the arbitral tribunal ruled that the contract between the Claimant and the Respondent was a secret commission agreement which constituted a particularly offensive violation of the rights of a third party (party D) to the proper performance of the fiduciary duties owed to it by the engineer. The contract between Claimant and Respondent was therefore declared null and void according to Swiss law. Pursuant to Swiss law, the secret commission did in fact constitute not only a "traitor's reward" through "bribes" or "corruption money" or "kickbacks," but also an intolerable breach of the distinct fiduciary obligations assumed by an architect/engineer towards an employer acting as principal. The arbitral tribunal added that Swiss law concerning secret commission agreements covering bribes was in accordance with international public policy requirements.

AWARD:

The arbitral tribunal rejected the Claimant's claim in its entirety.

PUBLISHED IN:

Yearbook Commercial Arbitration XIX (1994), p. 124.

12. ICC case no. 6286 of 1991 (partial award)

PARTIES:

Claimant: Consortium partner (US)
Respondents: Partner 1 and consortium leader (Germany), Partner 2 (Germany), Partner 3 (Germany) and Partner 4 (Canada)

PLACE OF ARBITRATION:

Geneva

LAW APPLICABLE TO THE MERITS:

Swiss law

SUBJECT MATTERS:

Revocation of management authority by a consortium partner.
Legality of consultancy agreements.
No proof of bribery.

SUMMARY OF FACTS:

The Claimant and all Respondents entered into an Operating Agreement
creating a consortium in order to exploit a raw materials concession granted
by the government of a Middle Eastern country. Under the Operating Agreement, the first Respondent was designated as manager (leader) for the joint
operation. In order to resolve certain issues related to the relationship
between the government and the consortium, the first Respondent, acting
in its capacity as Operator or leader, entered into several consultancy agreements, two of which were made with a Panamanian company as intermediary. The president of the Panamanian company was a diplomatic agent
of the Middle Eastern country. A dispute arose between the consortium
leader (Respondent) and one partner (Claimant), who revoked the authority
of the leader on the ground that it had allegedly concluded an illicit
consultancy agreement with the Panamanian intermediary. The Claimant
refused to pay its share of the intermediary's commission and initiated
arbitration proceedings against the other partners requesting dissolution of
the consortium and recovery of damages.

REASONING OF THE TRIBUNAL:

As to the required standard of proof, the arbitral tribunal ruled that proof of
bribery may be "adopted only if it is established that the amounts paid were
intended to bribe officials to trade on their influence to obtain favours."
Corruption was not proved, since it was not established that the beneficiary
(the Panamanian intermediary) of the commission "had effectively played
a part in respect of the concessions. On the contrary, the concessions have
not been granted yet, as the Government continues the negotiation only as
a result of a decision of arbitral nature." Moreover, the arbitral tribunal found
that the amounts pertaining to the agreements with the intermediary were
never paid. Hence, no corruption could have been committed.

AWARD:

The arbitral tribunal held that the first Respondent had behaved legally and
that its management authority had not been validly revoked by the Claimant.

PUBLISHED IN:

Yearbook Commercial Arbitration XIX (1994), p. 141.

13. ICC case no. 6401 of 1990/1991 (Westinghouse)

PARTIES:

Claimants: Westinghouse and Burns & Roe (US)
Respondents: National Power Co. and the Republic of the Philippines

PLACE OF ARBITRATION:

Geneva

LAW APPLICABLE TO THE MERITS:

Swiss law

SUBJECT MATTERS:

High standard of proof required in order to establish corruption.
No evidence of bribery.

SUMMARY OF FACTS:

National Power Co. of Philippines agreed upon two engineering and consulting contracts, one with Westinghouse and one with Burns & Roe, concerning the construction of a nuclear plant in the Philippines. In order to obtain the award, Westinghouse paid commissions to an associate of the former President Ferdinand E. Marcos. The associate acted as local agent for both Claimants. The dispute arose when the Claimants sought recovery of certain outstanding claims, but the two Respondents denied payment on the ground that the Claimants had paid bribery money to the former President Marcos.

REASONING OF THE TRIBUNAL:

The arbitral tribunal discussed the required standard of proof. It held that the standard to be applied in weighing the evidence was the "preponderance of evidence" standard as generally understood in the three states of the parties (the Philippines, New Jersey and Pennsylvania). With respect to the allegation of corruption, a higher standard of "clear and convincing evidence" would however apply: fraud in civil (as compared to criminal) cases must be proven to exist by clear and convincing evidence amounting to more than a mere preponderance, and cannot be justified by mere speculation. Even though evidence existed that Westinghouse intended to bribe President Marcos by paying the local agent, the arbitral tribunal stated that the Respondents failed to carry their burden of proof, since they neither provided evidence of payments to Marcos nor proved the existence of an agreement between President Marcos and Westinghouse.

AWARD:

The arbitral tribunal stated that the (main) contracts were valid and rejected any allegation of bribery.

US COURTS' DECISIONS:

> The Respondents also filed multiple tort and contract claims with the US Courts. The US District Court for the District of New Jersey held that the standard of proof applied by the ICC arbitral tribunal was different from the standard applied by a state court. According to the Court, the ICC arbitral tribunal "applied a significantly heavier burden of proof than would be applied at trial." The Court added that "by compartmentalizing and segregating the categories of evidence the Tribunal deprived it as a whole of its natural collective force in a way in which the evidence might not be so deprived in this Court." As a result, the judge ruled that "there is ample evidence to permit a reasonable jury to find that the [local agent's] commissions were intended to be paid in whole or in part to President Marcos and were in fact paid in whole or in part to him or upon his direction."

> The judge did not criticize the conclusions in the ICC award. He stressed that the ICC tribunal "was considering somewhat different issues and applying a different standard of proof."

MENTIONED BY:

> Mealey Publications, February 1992, Vol. 7, pp. 3 and A-1; Matthias Scherrer, "Circumstantial Evidence in Corruption Cases Before International Arbitral Tribunals," *International Arbitration Law Review, 2002*, pp. 29; *Journal du Droit International,* 1996, p. 1056 (Ruling on the procedure to be followed); *Journal du Droit International,* 1998, p. 1058 (Ruling on the procedure to be followed, comment by D. H.).

14. ICSID case no. ARB/84/3 of May 1992

PARTIES:

> Claimants: Southern Pacific Properties (Middle East) Limited (Hong Kong) and Southern Pacific Properties Limited (Hong Kong)
> Respondent: The Arab Republic of Egypt

SUBJECT MATTER:

> No proof of corruption

SUMMARY OF FACTS:

> The parties were involved in a joint venture intended to develop two international tourist projects at the Pyramids area in Cairo. Disputes arose as to the obligations of the Respondent and compensation to the Claimants for cancellation of the investment project.

AWARD:

> Among various other contentions, the Respondent's pleadings contained repeated allusions to irregular contacts and improper business connections on the part of the Claimants. The Respondent also alleged that certain

former Government servants were employed by the Claimants and that the Claimants by-passed normal Government channels of communication and "went right to the top." On these grounds, the Respondent requested the Tribunal to declare that the Claimants' claims were (translation) "unfounded by reason of the corruption revealed by the actions of SPP and SPP (ME)."

However, the Tribunal found that the allusions were "not supported by the evidence in the record and are based on suppositions [...]. On such grounds, it is simply not possible to reach the findings of fact and conclusions requested by the Respondent."

In particular, the Tribunal noted that the Respondent admitted the lack of concrete evidence in this respect when, on request of the Tribunal, the Respondent stated that "nothing we have said in our memorials should be construed as an accusation, or allegation of misconduct regarding any particular Egyptian Official referred to [...]" and the particular persons whom the Respondent had exempted from any allegation of misconduct were the very same persons who established the initial contacts with the Claimants.

PUBLISHED IN:

Yearbook Commercial Arbitration XIX 1994, p. 51; *International Legal Materials,* 1993, p. 933

15. ICC case no. 6474 of 1992: partial award on jurisdiction

PARTIES:

Claimant: Supplier from a European country
Respondent: State X

PLACE OF ARBITRATION:

Zurich

LAW APPLICABLE TO THE MERITS:

Swiss law

SUBJECT MATTERS:

Arbitration clause valid notwithstanding an allegation of fraud or corruption affecting the validity of the contract containing the clause.

The arbitration clause as such could be invalid if it were proved that such clause was induced by corruption and fraud.

SUMMARY OF FACTS:

A European supplier entered into several contracts to supply agricultural products to the Republic of X. A dispute arose, and the Claimant initiated arbitration relying on the ICC arbitration clause contained in the contracts. The Respondent objected to jurisdiction on the ground that the contract was induced by corruption and fraud.

AWARD ON JURISDICTION:

According to the arbitral tribunal, in the context of a discussion of jurisdiction, it must be alleged and shown through proper evidence that the arbitration clause "was entered into solely because of corruption and fraud." In the present case, the arbitral tribunal found that not even a prima facie case of corruption, fraud or illegality (possibly invalidating the arbitration clause) on the part of the government officials had been established by the Respondent.

The question of whether corruption and fraud were present and, in the affirmative, the issue of their effects upon the validity of the contracts in general were not decided in this partial award and were reserved for a further award.

The arbitral tribunal decided that it had jurisdiction and that the claims were admissible.

PUBLISHED IN:

Yearbook Commercial Arbitration XXV (2000), p. 279

16. ICC case of March 31, 1992

PARTIES:

Claimant: Westman International Ltd. (UK)
Respondent: European Gas Turbines SA (France)

PLACE OF ARBITRATION:

Paris

LAW APPLICABLE TO THE MERITS:

French law

SUBJECT MATTERS:

Contract contrary to French international public policy and to the ethics of international business due to the fact that it results from and has the purpose of selling influence and paying bribes.
Lack of proof.

SUMMARY OF FACTS:

In the context of a petrochemical project in Iran, the Respondent entered into an agreement with the Claimant under which the Claimant was to promote the sale of the Respondent's gas turbines in Iran, transmit as much information as possible and provide useful advice for obtaining a contract under the best possible conditions. The agreement provided for the payment to the Claimant of a commission that was to cover (translation) "all expenses of any nature whatsoever that the Claimant may have to incur to carry out its duties." It was also stipulated that the commission would not be due if the Respondent did not receive any contracts during the term of the agreement.

The Respondent was pre-qualified before the expiration of the agreement, but the order for the gas turbines was signed by the owner only after the expiration of the agreement. The Respondent refused to pay the commission to the Claimant.

AWARD:

The arbitral tribunal concluded, primarily, that a valid contract existed between the parties and declared that it was not apparent from the terms of the contract that the Claimant had to exercise influence with the owner to obtain the pre-qualification of the Respondent. Its role was solely to (translation) "promote the Respondent's gas turbines." During the proceedings, the Claimant produced a statement of its expenses, including notably the payment of its personnel and its general expenses.

The Respondent was ordered to pay the agreed commission, that is, 4% of the amount of the supply contract.

DECISION OF THE PARIS:

The Respondent sought the annulment of the arbitral.

COURT OF APPEAL

Award before the Paris Court of Appeal, following a complaint that the arbitrators had considered as valid an international brokerage agreement that was prohibited by the law of the importing State. The Court decided that neither the agreement, the parties' behavior, the existence of a Swiss bank account into which the commission was to have been paid, nor the fact that the Claimant did not report on all the services provided by it, constituted facts supporting the supposition that there was a sale of influence under French law, which the arbitrators were required to apply. The arbitral award was in the end partially annulled, but not on the grounds of corruption.

PUBLISHED IN:

The arbitral award is not published. Only the decision of the Paris Court of Appeals, mentioning the award, is published in the *Revue de l'Arbitrage*, 1994, p. 359, and in *Bulletin A.S.A.*, 1994, p. 105 (with a summary by Adel Nassar).

17. ICC award of 1993

ARBITRAL TRIBUNAL:

Sole arbitrator

PARTIES:

Claimant: X
Respondent: Y

PLACE OF ARBITRATION:

Geneva

LAW APPLICABLE TO THE MERITS:

French law

AWARD:

No direct or circumstantial evidence of bribery. Y was ordered to pay to X the 5% commission agreed in the contract.

MENTIONED BY:

Matthias Scherer, "Circumstantial Evidence in Corruption Cases Before International Arbitral Tribunals," *International Arbitration Law Review,* 2002, p. 29 (*A.S.A. Bulletin,* 1998, pp. 210, 442)

18. ICC case no. 6497 of 1994

PARTIES:

Claimant: Consultant (Liechtenstein)
Respondent: Contractor (Germany)

PLACE OF ARBITRATION:

Geneva

LAW APPLICABLE TO THE MERITS:

Swiss law

SUBJECT MATTERS:

Multiple "consultancy" agreements.
What standard of proof applies to prove bribery?
What evidence is admissible?
Absence of proof for most of the agreements.
Sufficient degree of probability of bribery in one of the agreements.

SUMMARY OF FACTS:

Over a period of approximately ten years, the parties entered into a number of consultancy agreements. The main purpose of those agreements was for the Claimant to assist the Respondent in obtaining construction contracts in a number of countries, including a certain Middle Eastern country. In addition to these basic agreements, the parties entered into a great number of specific agreements providing for additional remuneration (up to 5.5%), as well as, in some cases, additional services to be charged to the Claimant. Claimant later sought the payment of the amount due in relation to several contracts awarded to the Respondent. The Respondent refused and the Claimant initiated arbitration. The Respondent contested the claim on the ground that the real purpose of all the agreements was to bribe officials in the Middle Eastern country.

REASONING OF THE TRIBUNAL:

According to the arbitral tribunal, the party alleging bribery bears the burden of proof, a burden that, in normal circumstances, cannot be shifted to the arbitrators or to the other party. A civil court, and in particular an arbitral tribunal, has no power to make an official inquiry and has no duty to search independently for the truth. If the demonstration of the party making the allegations is not convincing, the tribunal should reject its argument, even if the tribunal has some doubts about whether the agreements involved bribery. In this case, the Respondent failed to prove conclusively that the real purpose of the agreements was bribery. Considering that the Respondent elected not to disclose the names of the many beneficiaries, which it allegedly knew, it was deemed inappropriate to shift the burden of proof to Claimant. Shifting the burden of proof to the Claimant could be justified if only the Claimant holds the proof, in which case the Claimant could be ordered to disclose that evidence, but such circumstances were not present in the case in point. The arbitral tribunal then found that "although the amounts paid to Claimant were very high, and the effective costs of Claimant have been only a small fraction of such amount, such payment was not perceived as being abnormal for a consultancy agreement, without any bribery nature."

Although this was the reasoning for most of the consultancy agreements, the tribunal found that, in relation to one specific consultancy agreement, a high enough degree of probability existed that its real purpose was to channel bribes to officials in country X for this to be considered a case of bribery. The reasons why the tribunal singled out that specific agreement were: (a) the circumstances surrounding the conclusion of the agreement, (b) the extraordinary size of the commission (33.33%), which was considered "extremely unusual" and (c) the fact that the Claimant himself did not contest that the agreement in question was null and void under Swiss law if the tribunal reached the conclusion that there was a high degree of probability that its real purpose was to corrupt officials in country X having the power to decide upon the award of the contract to the Respondent and upon the payment to the Respondent of the sums mentioned in the contract.

AWARD:

The tribunal accepted the claims, except in the case of the specific agreement which was declared null and void as having been induced by bribery.

PUBLISHED IN:

Yearbook Commercial Arbitration XXIV (1999), p. 71.

19. ICC case no. 7047 of 1994

PARTIES:

Claimant: Consultant (State Y)
Respondents: State agency (State Z) and State owned bank (State Z)

PLACE OF ARBITRATION:

Geneva

LAW APPLICABLE TO THE MERITS:

Swiss law

SUBJECT MATTERS:

Evidence of bribery.
Burden of proof.
Required standard of proof.
No violation of the mandatory provisions of the importing State.

SUMMARY OF FACTS:

The parties entered into a contract under which Claimant undertook to consult, advise and otherwise assist Respondent in promoting and selling Respondent's military products and services to State X. The agreement provided, *inter alia*, that any contracts that Respondent entered into during the term of the agreement with third parties in State X were to be considered conclusively and irrefutably the result of the efforts of the Claimant. Later on, the Respondent and a representative of State X signed a contract for the sale of military products (main contract). Prior to signing of main contract, the representative of State X sent to Respondent a public circular advising that contracts for the delivery of arms or other military devices must be concluded directly with representatives of State X without any participation of agents or intermediaries. After receiving of the circular, the Respondent sent it to the Claimant, expressing its wish to terminate the brokerage agreement since it had become impossible to perform it. The Claimant refused the termination and initiated arbitration.

The arbitral tribunal found the agreement to be a valid brokerage contract. Even though bribery renders an agreement invalid, bribery is a fact which, in arbitration proceedings, must be alleged and for which evidence must be submitted by the party making the allegation. Furthermore, the tribunal must be convinced that there is indeed a case of bribery. "A mere suspicion by any member of the arbitral tribunal, communicated neither to the parties nor to the witness during the phase to establish the facts of the case, is entirely insufficient to form such a conviction of the arbitral tribunal." The Respondent did not allege that the parties jointly had intended that illicit means be used by the Claimant, nor did the evidence submitted to the arbitral tribunal convince it of such intention. The clause in the agreement which exonerated the Claimant from proving his actual services might in principal imply a joint illicit intention, but in the case under consideration, the clause was not by itself sufficient to prove an illicit intention since the post-contractual correspondence between Claimant and Respondent showed that the Claimant did indeed provide the promised services. The tribunal further held that the amount of fees agreed upon also failed to show joint illicit intentions. The only assertion made by the Respondent – that the stipulated fees were disproportionately high – was not sufficient to invalidate the agreement.

The arbitral tribunal did not consider any potential effect of the circular on the agreement, since the Respondent did not prove that the circular was part of the mandatory law of State X, nor did it specify the mandatory provisions on which the circular was based.

AWARD:
The arbitral tribunal accepted the claim.

PUBLISHED IN:
Yearbook Commercial Arbitration XXI (1996), p. 79

20. *Ad Hoc* award of July 28, 1995

PARTIES:
Claimant: Company from Panama
Respondent: Z

PLACE OF ARBITRATION:
Choppet, Switzerland

LAW APPLICABLE TO THE MERITS:
Swiss law

SUBJECT MATTER:
Bribery alleged but not evidenced.

AWARD:
The fact that the Claimant made payments to a third party did not breach the contract between Claimant and the Respondent and did not constitute proof of bribery. The rendering of services by the consultant was undisputed.

MENTIONED BY:
Matthias Scherer, "Circumstantial Evidence in Corruption Cases Before International Arbitral Tribunals," *International Arbitration Law Review*, 2002, p. 29 (*A.S.A. Bulletin*, 1995, p. 742).

21. ICC case no. 7664 of 1996

PARTIES:

Claimant: Frontier AG & Brunner Soc.
Respondent: Thomson CSF

PLACE OF ARBITRATION:

Geneva

APPLICABLE LAW TO THE MERITS:

French law

AWARD:

Even though an agent was paid to attempt to influence Chinese authorities so that they would not object to the sale of war ships to Taiwan, no evidence of bribery was found. The agency contract was declared valid.

The award was confirmed by the Swiss Federal Tribunal on January 28, 1997 (*A.S.A. Bulletin,* 1998, p. 118).

MENTIONED BY:

Matthias Scherer, "Circumstantial Evidence in Corruption Cases Before International Arbitral Tribunals," *International Arbitration Law Review,* 2002, p. 29

22. ICC case no. 8113 of 1996

PARTIES:

Claimant: Contractor (France)
Respondent: Agent (South-East Asian country)

PLACE OF ARBITRATION:

Lausanne

LAW APPLICABLE TO THE MERITS:

French law

AWARD:

No allegation of bribery was raised, even though the commission was stipulated to be 8.25% of the contract amount. Fee reduced by the arbitral tribunal for being excessive in light of services rendered.

MENTIONED BY:

Matthias Scherer, "Circumstantial Evidence in Corruption Cases Before International Arbitral Tribunals," *International Arbitration Law Review,* 2002, p. 29 *ICC Bulletin,* Spring 2001, p. 85

23. ICC case no. 8891 of 1998

PARTIES:

Claimant: Consultant
Respondent: Exporter to State X

SUBJECT MATTERS:

Legal sources (national or international) establishing the validity of the consultancy agreement in question.
Application of "four indicia" to prove illegality.

SUMMARY OF FACTS:

The parties concluded a consultancy contract under which the Claimant had to assist the Respondent in obtaining an increase in the price of two contracts which the Respondent had already concluded with State X.

REASONING OF THE TRIBUNAL:

The arbitral tribunal started by declaring that the illegality of contracts establishing bribery is well recognized by arbitral tribunals, which usually apply national law as their primary source and refer to international general principles as a supplementary source. The tribunal in this case preferred to give precedence to international sources.

Concerning the difficulty of proving illegality, the arbitral tribunal stated that there were four indicia on the basis of which an arbitral tribunal may, in general terms, base its assumption of illegality:
a) the inability of the agent to provide evidentiary proof of his activities,
b) the duration of the agent's intervention,
c) the manner and method of remunerating the agent, and
d) the amount of money agreed to be payable to the agent as compared to the advantages obtained by the principal.

After listing the above standards or indices, the arbitral tribunal applied them to the case in question and concluded that the consultancy contract was entered into with the intent of conducting bribery and was to be declared, pursuant to international public policy, null and void.

AWARD:

The arbitral tribunal rejected the claim.

PUBLISHED IN:

Journal du Droit International, 2000, p. 1076

24. ICC case no. 9333 of 1998

ARBITRAL TRIBUNAL:

Sole arbitrator

PARTIES:
> Claimant: Agent (Morocco)
> Respondent: Contractor (France)

PLACE OF ARBITRATION:
> Geneva

LAW APPLICABLE TO THE MERITS:
> Swiss law

SUBJECT MATTERS:
> No proof of corruption.
> No violation of foreign law in contravention of moral standards under Swiss law.

SUMMARY OF FACTS:
> The parties had concluded an agency agreement under which the Claimant was to provide services aimed at assisting the Respondent in obtaining a construction contract. The remuneration of the Claimant was paid via a commission. The Respondent is part of an American group and was thus prohibited, under the laws of the United States, from paying commissions to an agent into an account located in a country other than the agent's country and different from the place where the services were rendered. Invoking this prohibition, the Respondent refused to pay the Claimant, on the basis that the Claimant's bank accounts were located in Switzerland.

REASONING OF THE TRIBUNAL:
> Under exceptional circumstances, a violation of a foreign law may be considered as contrary to moral standards under Swiss law, if it is irreconcilable with Swiss moral standards. In the case under consideration, a violation of the US Foreign Corrupt Practices Act (FCPA) was not established, because (translation) "the ground of corruption was not established by evidence ...."

> Moreover, the FCPA does not apply to American subsidiaries located abroad, nor may it prevail over the choice of another substantive law made by the parties merely because of the (translation) "powerful and legitimate interest of the United States in applying this law." In this respect, the arbitrator declared that it (translation) "would be slightly inappropriate to apply in this manner the FCPA to companies located outside the United States (...) the fight against corruption, to be sure a laudable objective, not necessarily justifying the exportation of the singular methods or code of conduct of the FCPA to achieve this objective (...)."

AWARD:
> The arbitrator accepted the claim for payment of commissions.

PUBLISHED IN:
> *ICC International Court of Arbitration Bulletin,* 1999, Vol. 10, p. 102

25. Award of May 4, 1999 in an ad-hoc UNCITRAL arbitration

PARTIES:

Claimant: Himpurna California Energy Ltd. (Bermuda)
Respondent: PT. (Persero) Persuahaan Listruik Negara (Indonesia)

PLACE OF ARBITRATION:

Jakarta, Indonesia

LAW APPLICABLE TO THE MERITS:

Indonesian law

SUBJECT MATTERS:

No violation of mandatory provisions.
No evidence of bribery.

SUMMARY OF FACTS:

The Claimant entered into an energy sales contract with an Indonesian state-owned electricity enterprise (Respondent) to explore and develop geothermal resources in Indonesia. Pursuant to the contract, the Claimant was to build two power plants in Indonesia and to sell the power to the Respondent. Since the Respondent failed to purchase the power, the Claimant initiated arbitration.

AWARD OF MAY 4:

Among the various arguments raised by the Respondent, one concerned the alleged illegality of the energy sales contract due to: (a) non-compliance with mandatory provisions of Indonesian law and (b) an allegation of corruption in the conclusion of the Contract.

The arbitral tribunal stated that it is "contrary to experience that a State-owned institution [...], whose director is appointed directly by the Head of State, engages in activities contrary to the mandatory law of that country."

Furthermore, "[...] such a posture puts into question the reliability of undertakings of the country in question [...] when a country's reputation as a contractual partner suffers, the terms on which it is able to attract foreign investment and financing are impaired."

As to the allegation of corruption, the arbitral tribunal stated that "[...] a finding of illegality or other invalidity must not be made lightly, but must be supported by clear and convincing proof [...]," which was not provided here.

In addition, the tribunal declared that the arbitrators "would rigorously oppose any attempts to use the arbitral process to give effect to contracts contaminated by corruption. But such grave accusations must be proven."

PUBLISHED IN:

Yearbook Commercial Arbitration XXV (2000), p. 13; *Mealey's International Arbitration Report,* Dec. 1999, p. A-1

BIBLIOGRAPHY

Arfazadeh, Homayoon, "Considérations pragmatiques sur la compétence respective de l'arbitre et du juge en matière de corruption", *A.S.A. Bulletin*, 2001, p. 672;

Association Française d'Arbitrage, "L'Arbitrage et la Corruption", Colloquium of 27 September 1995 at the Chamber of Commerce and Industry in Paris;

Bolle, Pierre-Hewis, "Pratique de corruption et transactions commerciales internationales", *Revue Critique de Droit International Privé*, 1982, p. 339;

Brown, Ewan, "Illegality and Public Policy – Enforcement of Arbitral Awards in England: *Hilmarton Limited v. Omnium de Traitement et de Valorisation S.A.*", *International Arbitration Law Review*, 2000, p. 31;

Derains, Yves, "Les Tendances de la Jurisprudence Arbitrale Internationale", *Journal du Droit International*, 1993, p. 846;

Derains, Yves, "Analyse de Sentences Arbitrales, Les commissions illicites", Institut du Droit et des Pratiques des Affaires Internationale d'ICC, ICC Publication 480/2, Paris 1992, p. 61;

Derains, Yves, "La lutte contre la corruption – Le point de vue de l'arbitre international", in Contribution to the 34th AIJA Congress Montreux 1996, p. 9;

El Kosheri, Ahmed S. and Leboulanger, Philippe, "L'arbitrage face à la Corruption et aux Trafics d'influence", *Revue de l'Arbitrage*, 1984, p. 3;

Eriksson, Magnus, "Arbitration and Contracts involving corrupt practices: The arbitrator's Dilemma", *American Review of International Arbitration*, 1993, p. 371;

Fadlallah, Ibrahim, "Les instruments de l'illicité, L'illicité dans le commerce international", under the direction of P. Kahn and C. Kessedjian, Paris 1996, p. 292;

Giardina, Andrea, "Norme imperative contro le intermediazioni nei contratti ed arbitrato internazionale", *Rivista dell'Arbitrato*, 1992, p. 784;

Giardina, Andrea, "Riconoscimento in Francia di lodi esteri annullati nel paese d'origine", *Rivista dell'Arbitrato*, 1997, p. 394;

Hardey, Tim, "Corruption in International Trade", *The McKenna Law Letter*, 1994, p.21;

Heuzé, Vincent, "La Morale, l'Arbitre et le juge", *Revue de l'Arbitrage*, 1993, p. 179;

Hochstrasser, Daniel, "Choice of Law and 'Foreign' Mandatory Rules in Inter-national Arbitration," World Trade and Arbitration Materials, 1994, p. 57;

Knoepfler, "Corruption et arbitrage international, Les contrats de distribution", Contributions made to Professeur Dessemontet, Publication CEDIDAC, Lausanne 1998, p. 359;

Lalive, Pierre, "Ordre Public Transnational (ou réellement international) et Arbitrage International", *Revue de l'Arbitrage*, 1986, p. 329;

Lamethe, Didier, "L'illicité en matière des services liés au commerce international, L'illicité dans le commerce international", under the direction of P. Kahn and C. Kessedjian, Paris 1996, p. 177;

Lew, Julian D.M., "Contemporary Problems", *International Arbitration*, 1987, p. 82;

Lombardini, Carlo, "Corruption et blanchiment", *Anwaltsrevue*, 2001, p. 7;

Mayer, P. "Le contrat illicite", *Revue de l'Arbitrage* 1984, p. 205;

Mebroukine, Ali, "Le choix de la Suisse comme siège de l'arbitrage dans les clauses d'arbitrage conclues entre entreprises algériennes et entreprises étrangères", *A.S.A. Bulletin*, 1995, p. 4;

Nasser, Adel, "Ordre public international et arbitrage ? Y a-t-il eu une évolution?", *A.S.A. Bulletin*, 1994, p. 110;

Oppetit, Bruno, "Le paradoxe de la corruption à l'épreuve du droit du commerce international", *Journal du Droit International*, 1987, p. 5;

Reiner, Andreas, "The Standards and Burden of Proof in International Arbitration", *Arbitration International*, 1994, p. 336;

Rosell, J. and Prager, H., "Illicit Commissions and International Arbitration, The Question of Proof", *International Arbitration*, 1999, p. 329;

Sayed, Abdulhay, "Corruption in International Trade and Commercial Arbitration", Thesis No. 613, Geneva 2001;

Sayed, Abdulhay, "La question de la corruption dans l'arbitrage commercial international: Inventaire des solutions", *A.S.A. Bulletin*, 2001, p. 653;

Scherer, Matthias, "Beweisfragen bei Korruptionsfällen vor internationalen Schiedsgerichten", *A.S.A. Bulletin*, 2001, p. 684;

Scherer, Matthias, "International Arbitration and corruption – Synopsis of selected arbitral awards", *A.S.A. Bulletin*, 2001, p. 710;

Scherer, Matthias, "Circumstantial Evidence in Corruption Cases Before International Arbitral Tribunals", *International Arbitration Law Review*, 2002, p. 29;

Wetter, Gillis, "Issues of corruption before international arbitral tribunals: The authentic text and true meaning of Judge Gunnar Lagergren's 1963 Award in ICC Case No. 1110", *Arbitration International*, 1994, p. 277.

8

Arbitration - money laundering, corruption and fraud:
The role of the tribunals

By Allan Philip
Advocate, Professor dr. jur., Philip & Partners,
Copenhagen, Denmark;
Honorary Council Member, ICC Institute of World Business Law

INTRODUCTION

The issues that shall be discussed in the following paper are: How far is the Tribunal entitled or bound to take into account issues of money laundering, corruption and fraud? If such issues are not pleaded, is there a danger of the Tribunal acting *ultra petita*? What is the enforceability of awards which contain findings relating to such issues.

It is the starting point that money laundering, corruption and fraud are criminal activities. Differences exist among writers and arbitrators as to how arbitral tribunals ought to react if and when they realize that they are faced with such activities in the case before them.

Some arbitrators and writers have taken the position that they do not have jurisdiction in such cases, because the claims are not arbitrable, or, which amounts to the same thing, because the claims are contrary to public policy or good morals.

Others have considered that the doctrine of the separability of the arbitration clause leads to the result that they do have jurisdiction and have to decide the merits of the case and take any illegality resulting from the criminal activity into consideration when they decide the case. The latter seems to be the dominant view today, although some writers still adhere to the former view.

Personally, I believe that either view is too much of a generalization. There may certainly be cases in which it is abundantly clear from the beginning that the whole case on both sides is of such a nature that no honest arbitrator can touch it. Whether one should refer to international public policy, morals or something else is an open problem. What is international public policy anyway? Is there such a thing, or is it left to each arbitrator to formulate his own? There seems to be consensus that, in principle, arbitrators are not bound by the international public policy or public policy generally of a particular forum, such as, e.g., that of the seat of arbitration.

In most cases, the matter will be more complicated and the issue relating to money laundering, bribery or fraud may be a side issue or may only relate to the case of one side in the arbitration, or, finally may only be revealed little by little or at a late stage in the proceedings. In such circumstances, it may be better to take jurisdiction, decide such issues as are not tainted by illegality and either refuse to deal with the other issues or decide them on the basis that the claim or defence is illegal.

By going into the substance of the claim and refusing to admit it because of its illegality, one often arrives at the same result as by refusing to take jurisdiction. A closer look at the famous award of Judge Lagergren, to which I shall come back, shows that, in fact, that is what he did, although he couched it in terms of a refusal to take jurisdiction.

1. IS THE ARBITRAL TRIBUNAL ENTITLED OR BOUND TO TAKE INTO ACCOUNT ISSUES OF MONEY LAUNDERING, CORRUPTION AND FRAUD?

So much by way of introduction. The first question that is raised is, whether the Arbitral Tribunal is entitled or bound to take into account issues of money laundering, corruption and fraud, that is, apply rules prohibiting such activities, whether found in the law applicable to the case or in some other law.

I think that we should not make too-general rules but rather have to look at specific situations to see how these issues arise in the individual case. I also think that we have to take into account that the three subjects mentioned above are not the only ones where problems of this nature may arise. As an example, it may be mentioned that breach of competition laws may give rise to exactly the same considerations, as became clear in the Eco Swiss case before the European Court of Justice, to which I shall come back. One may also mention illegal traffic in drugs, weapons or cultural goods and acts relating to terrorism[1]. Such cases, like those being discussed here, also have both a criminal law and a civil law side. It seems that an increasing number of cases involving the civil law side of competition or antitrust matters, such as the validity of contracts, are being decided by arbitral tribunals. This should be kept in mind.

The Lagergren case[2] is illustrative. The Award is by Judge Gunnar Lagergren, later for many years president of the Iran-US Claims Tribunal. One gets the impression from the references to it in various writings that he just threw a glance at the case, realized its character and stated that this was not a case he would handle. That is not so.

The case was between an Argentine person, Mr X, and an apparently British company, engaged in the manufacture of electrical equipment and wishing to sell such equipment to the Argentine Government. The company agreed with Mr X that he should promote the company's interest in this matter against the payment of a commission. The company did not get the order in question but did obtain an order six years later. Mr X asked for his commission. The company, however, answered that the commission agreement only related to the first order and had lapsed. As no agreement could be reached, the parties made an agreement to submit their dispute to ICC arbitration. The parties exchanged several written pleadings, and a four-day-long hearing was held with the examination of a number of witnesses and oral argument by the parties. Only then Judge Lagergren, in his award, which is 12 printed pages long, decided that he must decline jurisdiction. But he did so only after a full discussion in the award of the substance of the case and after having stated as follows:

> "However, before involving good morals and public policy as barring parties from recourse to judicial or arbitral instances in settling their disputes care must be taken to see that one party is not thereby able to reap the fruits of his own dishonest conduct by enriching himself at the expense of the other."
> Which he then proceeded to do.

Thus, he did, in fact, decide the case, although couching it in terms of declining jurisdiction, by in fact, although not formally, refusing to order the company to pay money mainly intended for bribes, but ensuring that it was not thereby obtaining an unjust enrichment. He could have come to the exact same result by taking jurisdiction and expressly making those same decisions.

Lagergren's case was a simple one, but it illustrates that it is often only after thorough investigation that the criminal character of a case appears. Other cases may be much more complicated and the criminal character of that which lies behind the various actions, documents and other facts may not be easy to ascertain and only be possible to realize far into the proceedings. It may also be that only certain parts of a case and some of the claims are of a criminal character. Where there is fraud, may only be on one side and the other party may be the innocent person that is being defrauded. In some such cases, a general rule that the arbitrators have no jurisdiction may deprive the innocent person of his right of protection.

All of this counts in favour of usually not declining jurisdiction but rather refusing to grant any claims which are of a criminal character or grant compensation where a party has been defrauded or otherwise deprived of its rights. Taking jurisdiction is, of course, not tantamount to accepting any claims that appear to be justified on the face of the contract, if the contract or the particular claim is clearly illegal. It means, e.g., accepting the claim by the other party that the contract is invalid because of its illegality.

That is what happened in the Loewe case[3], also named after the arbitrator, where contracts, intended to circumvent Yugoslav currency legislation and, on the basis of a fictitious contract, obtain bank credit, were declared null and void by the arbitrators, as claimed by one party.

It was mentioned at the beginning that at least some of those who argue that the arbitrators should decide the case do so with reference to the doctrine of separability: the contract may be invalid, but not the arbitration clause. This may apply in some cases. In the Lagergren case, the arbitration agreement was a subsequent submission agreement, concluded after the dispute had arisen and, therefore, clearly separable from the original agreement. In other cases the issues which are tainted by illegality may have nothing to do with the validity of the contract itself, but may relate to side issues. In any event, it seems better to rely on an analysis of the character of the cases than on a theoretical and legislative doctrine which does not have application in all cases. Where morals and international public policy are involved, that seems to be a very formal and technical approach.

In the Lagergren and Loewe cases, the arbitrators took into account issues respectively of corruption and fraud. Lagergren did so of his own motion. The Loewe Tribunal did it on the basis of a claim by a party. It does not seem to have given rise to criticism that Lagergren acted of his own motion for reasons of good morals and international public policy considerations.

But may arbitrators always do that? In arbitration as well as in the courts it is a generally recognized rule that the arbitrators may not go outside the claims by the parties, *ultra petita*. See e.g. Article V 1(c) of the New York Convention 1958, which provides for refusal of recognition and enforcement of the award if it deals with a difference which does not fall within the terms of the submission or contains decisions on matters beyond its scope. See also Articles 34 and 36 of the Model Law.

Where the question is one of jurisdiction, it seems accepted that generally a state court may act *ex officio*, although where both parties appear and neither raises the question of the existence of an arbitration agreement, a court may regard their behaviour as a waiver of the arbitration clause[4]. With respect to arbitration, failure by a party to object to the jurisdiction of the tribunal may and usually will be taken as a waiver of any objection; see, e.g., Article 33 of the ICC Rules. Therefore, arbitral tribunals will normally not raise issues of jurisdiction of their own motion.

The acceptance of the Lagergren award may, therefore, be based upon the view that the arbitral tribunal has an independent right to invoke good morals and international public policy, regardless of the claims of relief by the parties. But the Lagergren award was based purely on an issue of jurisdiction. It is necessary to discuss what the situation is if the arbitrator goes into the merits of the case and decides issues which have not been raised by the parties.

There is no doubt that, if a party raises as a defence on the merits that a contract is invalid or that a particular claim is unjustified because it is based on acts which amount to money laundering or bribery or fraudulent behaviour, the arbitrators may consider and decide that issue. But if no such defence is raised, can the arbitrators then raise the issue themselves and decide the claim on that basis?

The arbitrators must, no doubt, before taking such a step, raise the issue with the parties and hear their reactions, in particular why the party, who could have raised the defence earlier, now, when his attention is drawn to it, wishes to do so? Lagergren, in fact, did draw the parties' attention to the problem he saw. If this is not done, the award may suffer from another defect, viz. that the parties have not had due process, and recognition may be denied under Article V 1(b) of the New York Convention.

2. WHAT IF BOTH PARTIES REFUSE TO TAKE UP THE ISSUES?

But what if both parties refuse to take up the issue? Can the arbitrators then take it up of their own motion, call witnesses, and request the parties to address the issue?

The question has got new relevance as a result of the decision in the Eco Swiss case[5] of the European Court of Justice which concerns EU competition law. The case does not directly decide the issue, but it does give occasion to raise it also in that context, and it is illustrative of our problem.

The case concerned an award in an arbitration between Benetton and Eco Swiss. Somewhat simplified, what happened was, Benetton had terminated a license contract and distribution agreement, and Eco Swiss alleged that the termination was unlawful. Benetton was ordered in the award to pay a large amount in compensation to Eco Swiss, so it challenged the award in the Dutch courts and argued that the agreement was invalid because the agreement restricted competition and, therefore, was in breach of the prohibition in Article 81 of the EC treaty which invalidates agreements restricting competition. Benetton had not brought that defence in the arbitration, and the arbitral tribunal had not been aware of this possibility or, at least, had not raised it.

The Hoge Raad, the Dutch Supreme Court, found that it could not set aside the award on substantive grounds, as Dutch law is similar to the New York Convention. Only if Article 81 could be regarded as a rule of public policy would it be possible to set the award aside. However, the corresponding Dutch competition rules were not regarded as pertaining to Dutch public policy.

Therefore, the Dutch Court asked the EU Court for a preliminary judgement. The EU Court decided that Article 81 was a rule of European public policy (paragraph 39). It stated further that a national court on application must annul an award which is contrary to Article 81, if its domestic law requires it to annul an award which fails to observe national rules of public policy, whether they be competition rules or rules of another character (paragraphs 37 and 41 and paragraph 1 of the Ruling).

This raises the problem how arbitral tribunals shall act when they know that they are deciding a case where international public policy may result in annulment of the award if certain rules are not considered in the award or the award may otherwise be regarded as contrary to public policy. This question arises not only where competition law is concerned but in respect of any rules having a public policy character, such as the rules on money laundering, etc., that are discussed here. If the parties do not want the arbitrators to take up the issue and decide whether in some way the outcome would be different if they did, what shall the arbitratrors then do?

The decision of the Court of Justice does not answer or even raise that question. But it does give occasion to raise it. My own answer – but not everybody may agree with me – is, that arbitrators who become aware that such problems exist must raise them with the parties, to the extent possible obtain the necessary evidence and decide them. The arbitrators have a duty to make every effort to make sure that the award is enforceable at law, see, e.g., the ICC Rules Article 35. It must be admitted that with parties who are not willing to co-operate, that is not an easy task. It is, however, the duty of the arbitrators to establish the facts of the case by all appropriate means, cf. e.g. Article 20 of the ICC Rules.

In some cases, the problem may be solved more easily. If a party resists a claim on the basis of the invalidity of the underlying contract, but his grounds are insufficient, and the arbitrators find that he could have argued that the contract was tainted by fraud but did not do it, I believe that, whether he wishes to invoke fraud or not, the arbitrators may decide the case on that basis, provided they have raised the issue with the parties. This is a question of applying the law, not of going beyond the claims raised by the parties. *Jura novit curia*. The party has invoked the invalidity of the contract, only not the proper ground for it. That is then supplied by the arbitrators.

3.   THE APPLICABLE LAW

A special problem is the choice of the applicable law. Of course, failing a choice by the parties, the arbitrators today have very great freedom in that respect, cf. e.g. Article 17 of the ICC Rules. But where a particular law is chosen, can the arbitrators apply corruption or money laundering law of another country?

This possibility exists at least under Article 7 of the Rome Convention. It provides in paragraph 1 that in certain cases effect may be given to rules of law of another country than that, the law of which is otherwise applicable. That is so if under the law of that other country its rules of law must be applied in all cases, i.e. if those rules are internationally mandatory and thus are part of the international public policy of the country. This principle may, where necessary, i.e. where the arbitrators must otherwise apply a law by which certain activities are lawful, such as, e.g., bribery, be utilized if the arbitrators find that such activities should be stopped or not given recognition in a particular case.

4.   THE ENFORCEABILITY OF AWARDS

The final question is what is the enforceability of awards containing findings relating to such issues?

If the recognition or enforcement of an award would be contrary to public policy, it may be refused; see New York Convention, Article V 2 (b). It should not be forgotten that here we are talking about the public policy of the forum where enforcement is requested, not about an international public policy. The same is true if the subject matter of the dispute is not capable of settlement by arbitration under the law of that country; see Article V 2(a). Thus, awards whereby claims that are shown to rest on corruption, money laundering or fraud are admitted, may be set aside and refused recognition and enforcement by courts which do not accept such practices.

It should, however, be made clear that the provision in Article V 2 (b) does not say that the mere fact that the award contains findings on such issues results in its annulment. It depends on how the specific award decides the issues. If the award declares a contract for money laundering or a contract obtained by fraud invalid, it may well determine the consequences, such as compensation, restitution, etc.

Lagergren could have taken jurisdiction. He could have decided that, as a result of the invalidity of the contract, a party that had obtained unjust enrichment should pay the other party a sum of money. Loewe could have not only declared the Yugoslav contracts invalid but also decided on claims of compensation resulting therefrom. Such awards, although taking into account acts contrary to public policy, in their results would not be contrary to public policy and would, therefore, be enforceable[6].

FOOTNOTES

1   Cf. Lalive in ICCA Congress Series No. 3 1987 p. 284.

2   ICC case No. 1110/1963, printed in full as an annex to a comment to the case by Gillis Wetter in 10 Arbitration International (1994) 277, cf. also XXI Yearbook Commercial Arbitration (1996) 47, and Antonia Crivellaro above p. 119.

3   111 Journal du Droit International (Clunet) (1984) 914, also in Collection of ICC Arbitral Awards 1974-85, p. 490.

4   Cf. Fouchard, Gaillard, Goldman, On International Commercial Arbitration, 1999 p. 405.

5   Case C-126/97 [1999] ECR I 3055.

6   List of References:

   – Michael Bogdan; Book Review, 68 Nordic Journal of International Law (1999) p. 376

   – Magnus Eriksson, Arbitration and Contracts Involving Corrupt Practices: The Arbitrators Dilemma, IV The American Review of International Arbitration (1993) p. 371.

   – Berthold Goldman, The Complementary Roles of Judges and Arbitrators in Ensuring that International Commercial Arbitration is Effective, 60 Years of ICC Arbitration, 1984, pp 269 to 274.

   – Kaj Hobér, Extinctive Prescription and Applicable Law in Interstate Arbitration, 2001, p.128.

   – Pierre Lalive, Transnational (or Truly International) Public Policy and International Arbitration, ICCA Congress Series No. 3, 1987 p. 290.

   – Guiditta Cordero Moss, International Commercial Arbitration, 1999 p. 300.

   – Bruno Oppetit, Le Paradoxe de la corruption à l'épreuve du droit du commerce international.

   – Alan Redfern and Martin Hunter, Law and Practice of International Commercial Arbitration, Third Edition, 1999 p. 152.

9

Final remarks

By Robert Briner
Chairman, ICC International Court of Arbitration,
Paris, France

I would like to make a few remarks, in no particular order.

During this conference we repeatedly discussed the 40-year-old decision of Judge Lagergren. In deciding that the dispute was not arbitrable as a case of corruption was involved, Lagergren's decision is clearly out of date. You might perhaps say that this is the old English position: whenever a fraud is involved the matter is not arbitrable. But then, this position is not that old because the Supreme Court of Pakistan only recently decided exactly along the same lines in an ICC case. There have been one or two decisions where the Supreme Court of Pakistan decided that a case could not be decided by arbitration but had to be decided by the public courts as a party alleged that the contract, the subject of the dispute, had been obtained because of bribes paid to the previous government.

Perhaps there is some confusion in this debate. Using arbitration for laundering money seems to require an agreement between the parties. Such an agreement was mentioned in the discussions as a possibility in an award on agreed terms. Arbitrators, as well as to a certain degree arbitral institutions, should of course avoid being used as an instrument in such a process. Fortunately, cases where this might apply are rare.

Corruption is a different matter, and is not necessarily linked to money laundering. Indeed, they are two separate issues with regards to arbitration. First of all, one has to note that obviously not every agency contract is a contract to corrupt. Agents do provide valuable services and proper services, in sometimes very delicate circumstances.
In this connection, we are clearly no longer in the Lagergren environment. The

issue today is not whether the dispute is arbitral or not, but what does the applicable law say. The duty of arbitrators is to decide the case based on the applicable law or the rules of law which they deem to be appropriate. Of course, corruption has become something which is now considered to be against public order and therefore falls under Article V (2) b of the New York Convention.

The Eco Swiss and Benetton case was somewhat different because the European Court to a certain degree left the door open. As the Dutch courts had exhausted their internal proceedings reviewing the award and, notwithstanding that the award was against European public order, it could still be a valid arbitration decision. So it seems to be a problem of qualification, as the question is: if a violation of public order occurred, is the award then void or only voidable? With regards to antitrust matters, the question can perhaps be left open, especially when we are dealing with non-Western European parties, whereas corruption in all cases is considered to constitute a violation of international public order.

But then, of course, it comes down to the question of evidence. The arbitrators, for instance under the ICC rules, have the duty to establish the facts with all appropriate means as fast as possible. One often talks about negative inference etc. In reality, based on my experience, the question should be: what party carries the burden of proof for what allegations? Arbitrators sometimes seem to have difficulties in deciding this question clearly. Also in cases involving an allegation of corruption, one usually has a claimant who wants money from the other party. Obviously the question is: has the claimant brought the necessary evidence that the facts are such that it is entitled to the remedy it seeks, and does the applicable law allow this remedy? Fortunately, corruption does not often became an issue. I did not look at all the cases of Maître Crivellaro, but I thought his presentation was an excellent summary of them and it should not be all that difficult for arbitrators to establish the facts and apply the law to them.

In this connection, I would just like to make one closing comment regarding Article 35 of the ICC Rules. I would like to point out once more that this is a default provision, and not a primary, absolute rule. Article 35 says: "In all matters not expressly provided for in these rules, the arbitrator shall act in spirit of these Rules and shall make every effort to make sure that the award is enforceable at law." Therefore, it is not an absolute obligation for arbitrators to make awards that are enforceable. For one thing, we never know under what law awards will be enforced. You just have to go and look at Haliburton and Chromalloy. Many awards for proper legal reasons cannot be enforced in a particular country. Sometimes they do not need to be enforced at all and they are primarily needed, for instance, to allow an insurance company to pay to the winning party. It is therefore very dangerous to argue that Article 35 is a general rule that says arbitrators always have to see to it that they render an enforceable award because one cannot always really define what an enforceable award means.

Questions and answers

The 22nd Annual Meeting of the ICC Institute of World Business Law yielded a number of insightful, and sometimes provocative, observations from panellists and participants from the floor alike. Reproduced below, and in some cases translated from French, are a selection of the questions raised and the resultant discussion. For convenience, we have regrouped them by subject matter.

Please note that the tape and transcription of the "Questions and Answers" were in some cases incomplete or garbled. Our apologies to any participant whose words may have been misunderstood by us.

QUESTIONS ON DUTY TO REPORT

ANDREW W. A. BERKELEY

If I may take up the very last point made by Alan Jenkins and ask a paving question for this afternoon, where we will be concentrating on the duties of arbitrators. Alan made a point about the new duty, which is coming into force in England, to disclose suspicions of money laundering and he gave his point in relation to lawyer and client. For the purposes of paving the way for this afternoon, could I ask Alan and Kristine to say how much, if at all, do you think that might apply to an arbitrator, apart from as a lawyer and client?

SERGE LAZAREFF

That is the very purpose of today's meeting and I understand that these are the conclusions we should draw this afternoon. In other words, what we are trying to do this morning is to define at large the various money laundering issues, fraud, etc. Our objective is to know precisely what the arbitrator should do. We can say a few words now. But clearly it is the conclusion we want to reach tonight.

I would only point out one understatement of Mr. Jenkins when he said that the lawyer's duty to report might not be in the best interest of his client. I find that a very wonderful understatement.

KRISTINE KARSTEN

There is perhaps another issue, which is that even if you wish to report, it is not necessarily obvious that you will be able to do so. I address myself to those of you who may have tried to report things to the French authorities, the "TRACKFIN". They are responsible for collecting the declarations of suspicious activities. If you call up and you are not one of the regulated professions, they would basically not even want to take down your declaration. You are then down to the possibility of calling the public prosecutor who may instigate a criminal investigation. But that raises reporting to another level of responsibility and increases the reticence on the part of the non-regulated professionals.

SERGE LAZAREFF

This just shows that we are basically a very civilised country and that the basic problem is really the conflict of the ethical duty of the professional who takes an oath when he engages in his trade. I would be personally very concerned with the ethical duty. It is all very well for a civil servant to decide this or that. But I, who have a client who trusts me and who comes to me for advice, what should I do?

COMMENT FROM THE FLOOR

With regard to lawyers and other professionals making disclosures, the direct impact in the UK of the ludicrously small number of disclosures that have been made by the legal and accounting professions, who have had a duty to make disclosures since 1994 and who have routinely ignored that responsibility, has resulted in part in new legislation being introduced in the UK, with which it is increasingly more difficult to comply and which has now raised a much higher set of standards for the entire sector. I think there is a two-edged sword here, where, on the one hand, there is of necessity a need for lawyers to be able to consider their professional responsibilities. On the other hand, the UK government has made it perfectly clear that if that responsibility is not complied with, they will continue to ratchet up the standards with which we all now have to comply.

ALAN JENKINS

The first point made was that of the duty of care of the bank. That is traditionally owed to the customer of the bank, not to the person that the money is paid on to. But the question is not merely whether or not the bank should follow through on its suspicions. It may well have done so. What you often find in the UK is that a financial institution will make a report to the appropriate body in the UK, that is the national criminal intelligence service, which is a police body. The police will then in effect tell the institution what to do. It may say: "Carry on with the transaction so that we can follow the chain of events, so that we can see who is involved." So, the bank may have done all that it needed to do and all that it should have done, but is acting on police authority, in doing what it did. On the other hand, the risk is that it may not have recognised the suspicions for what they were and simply have acted upon its customer's instructions without reporting it to the police.

KRISTINE KARSTEN

There is another thing that you should know. In France, for example, it is a crime in itself to reveal to a third party that you have made a declaration. The purpose of this is that you do not want to tip off the fraudster, the money launderer or whatever that in fact there is an investigation going on.

BERNARDO M. CREMADES

We, the legal profession, have reacted to the second directive saying that, probably, in money laundering our profession is in danger. But now, there is another wave coming in the form of Sarbanes-Oxley. The question is not only for inside counsel, but also for the outside counsel. Once you are called to work on, let us say, a stock option scheme or any other plan a company has to prepare, are you obliged to make a report if you think that there is a crime after those corporate collapses have been taking place? What is going to happen? No manager will ever consult any legal professional, from the inside or outside, because the lawyer would be obliged to report, if this is what would be required. In the end, those decisions would be taken without legal advice, which is going to be worse than the situation in the US. What are the limits of this duty to report?

ALAN JENKINS

Firstly, I entirely agree with your concern about the attacks on the profession and the incursions into the professional secrecy obligations that we have. As to the limits on the duty to report suspicions of money laundering in the UK, essentially, there are none. The problem in the UK has been partly brought upon the legal profession by its own failure in the past to report suspicions of money laundering as we should have done. You may say that that in itself is undesirable, but the government and the parliament have decided that that is what we should have done. We have failed to do so and we have now landed ourselves, in common with other professions and businesses, with this very subjective standard. If we do not do what we are supposed to do now, they could send lawyers to jail. It has already happened under the old standard. It is a matter of very significant concern, but I do not have any solution. But I do think that the Americans are going too far in requiring lawyers to noisily blow the whistle in the US, in the circumstances that you have described.

COMMENT FROM THE FLOOR *(translated from the French)*

Indeed, the line between protecting the interests of your client and the reporting obligation is a very delicate issue. I agree with the preceding comments concerning the dangers for our democratic societies if lawyers can no longer act as an interface, if you reduce the possibility for more or less honest clients to express their concerns and request counsel from a professional. I think that we are going to lead people to create hidden networks, perhaps using lawyers. There will be individuals who will operate in the shadows of the ethical systems that, despite it all, characterize our bar associations in democratic countries. I think this is highly dangerous.

I wonder whether, perhaps, Switzerland may not have found a solution, for once, that is perhaps less troubling and that will cause fewer difficulties than that defined in the new European directive.

Fundamentally, in Switzerland, the idea is as follows: when you are a lawyer or a notary who is acting as a professional, the Penal Code obliges you to respect scrupulously professional secrecy. Naturally, ethical considerations require us – if we know that a client is going to use our advice for illicit purposes – to refrain from intervening, and most professionals will respect this principle. The question, to my mind, is not so much the profession as the activity being carried out. The Swiss lawyer or notary who carries out financial transactions, a little like portfolio managers or other professions, is not protected, is not constrained by professional secrecy. He is not acting, in this context, primarily as a lawyer or notary and, obviously, should be required to inform the equivalent of the French TRACFIN of his suspicions. I wonder whether this is not an avenue that should be more broadly explored.

KRISTINE KARSTEN *(translated from the French)*

It is probably a possible solution, in the abstract, but, unfortunately, I think that the steamroller of international legislation tends to go in the other direction. In France, today, and for that matter for the past several years, there is already an obligation imposed, in theory at least, on lawyers, but also on any other professional who acts in the context of transactions where there are cross-border movements of funds. There are two provisions in the law concerning the notification of suspicions. There is a long section imposing a specific duty to inform the authorities on a growing list of professionals, beginning with bankers and insurers and ending by jewelers and antiques dealers, including in the middle notaries and real estate agents.

Then there is a second section, much less well known, which says that any person who intervenes in a transaction implying cross-border movements of funds must file a declaration with the public prosecutor when he knows, and that is the key word, that the operation involves money laundering. This is the current state of the law in France.

But French law, which I know relatively well and which has always been consistent with European legislation, is going to be amended to take into account the most recent European directive, which contemplates a sort of judgement of Solomon separating the case of a lawyer acting as a defender of clients' rights from that of a lawyer acting as an advisor. In other words, if a money launderer asks me to defend him in a criminal action, I have an obligation to treat the matter as confidential. On the other hand, in the case evoked by Alan, where someone asks for advice, saying "Here's how the transaction will be structured. What do you think?" and if I am convinced that money laundering is involved, even if I have no proof of this, European law will oblige me to report my suspicions. Lawyers will have to develop split personalities.

ARTHUR HARVERD

If it would assist us here, I would just like to point out that, as far as English law is concerned on this matter, it is very simple. The English law, as it stands at the moment, says that any person who, through his job, office or profession, becomes suspicious that, in fact, a money laundering trans-action has taken place, he or she must disclose that fact. It is no longer a question of "may " or "has the opportunity to, if he so wishes." Under our law, as it now stands, if the information comes to that person through his job office or profession, he must disclose it.

SERGE LAZAREFF

There is no contradiction between what you both say. You both agree there is sort of offence under the law. What I understand is implied in what you said is that the law authorises you to do so, therefore you do it. But what should you do if there is no law? Would you consider that you have a duty to report an offence? Supposing, you were in a position where you would not have this text in your law, what would you do under English law in general?

COMMENT FROM THE FLOOR

I am getting increasingly confused about the European Union position in view of what we have heard from these two excellent presentations this morning. The European Community law is, I think, quite clear, and has been since the AM&S case 20 years ago, namely legal professional privilege is part of the *corpus juris* of the European Union. What inroads can be made to that? The European Union itself grappled with this question in the preamble to the directive made only last year in 2001. Let me just say that, having dealt with the problem, it concludes like this: "Legal advice has been made subject to the obligation of professional secrecy unless the legal counsellor is taking part in money laundering activities, the legal advice is provided for money laundering purposes or the lawyer knows that the client is seeking legal advice for money laundering purposes." You can summarise that by saying that if the lawyer is himself part of the money laundering scheme, then he must report himself and his client. But if he is not part of it, not only has he got no duty to report, but also in many countries, or some countries in the European Union, he is forbidden by law from reporting. I think, in light of those regimes which, unfortunately, at the beginning of the last century suffered under fascist governments and which used terrible means to extract information from lawyers, it is a criminal offence for a lawyer to breach his professional obligation.

I would hope that if English law goes ahead on the lines of what Alan Jenkins is telling us, someone will take it straight off to the court in Luxembourg and get this all right.

ALAN JENKINS

I agree with you. But in the way the law is being transposed into the U K, there may be a distinction to be made where a lawyer is instructed to defend somebody who is being investigated or charged with money laundering. Of course, by the time you have reached that point, if the client is being charged, the trail of suspicion has led to a charge. That is the distinction.

I think the problem in the UK is you may have unwittingly entered onto a transaction as a lawyer in which a client is buying a house and you see a chain of suspicious circumstances. It may just be, for example, that the client has decided he is not going to buy the house personally but he will buy the house using a company. And then, you will look at the company and you have to look at the factors that Kristine has talked about. In the light of the fact that we will have very shortly an objective standard, an English lawyer has no choice but to report his suspicions, if he has them or should have had them. That is the absolutely frightening consideration in England, Wales and Scotland now. Even if you do not have a suspicion, you are guilty of an offence if you should have a suspicion. It is so Orwellian.

COMMENT FROM THE FLOOR *(translated from the French)*

All this discussion of the obligation to declare your suspicions brings to my mind the mechanism that Italian legislators have put in place. Let me summarize it, since it may inspire others. Indeed, Italian legislators have made a distinction between money laundering and the crime of using money or assets of illegal origin. There is a 1991 law that defines a list of professionals that could (and the verb is expressed in the conditional tense) inform the Italian exchange control authorities (and not the penal authorities) that they suspect that money laundering is taking place. Arbitrators are not on this list.

I have the list in front of me: public employees, bank personnel, insurers, real estate intermediaries, fund managers, fiduciaries, stock market agents and other intermediaries that deal in financial transactions.

More generally, there is often, in our countries, an obligation for public employees to let the authorities know if they think a penal offense has occurred. It's part of the notion of public service, *l'incaricato di servicio publico*. I find it very disquieting, and I don't know what the answer is, that there might be a tendency to assimilate an arbitrator to an ordinary judge, on the basis that he is a substitute for a state judge. The situation becomes very confused. Is there not a risk that a local judge might say "true, the arbitrator is not a public employee, but he renders a public service and thus is obligated to declare his suspicions". Not to the administrative authorities, but to the penal authorities. I have been unable to find any decisions on this point.

COMMENT FROM THE FLOOR *(translated from the French)*

I'd like to raise a dissenting voice in response to the general tendency that today's debate is revealing. While money laundering may be a phenomenon that we should combat, money laundering flourishes in the places where confidentiality is the best respected. Bankers, who are perhaps less well equipped than lawyers or notaries to spot money laundering, are required to declare their suspicions. Obviously, the authorities have to decide whether to bring proceedings or not. But the professionals subject to these obligations can at least attempt to define what constitutes a "suspicion". If they can do that, we will have made some progress.

SERGE LAZAREFF

Thank you very much for raising these issues, which as I have mentioned raise moral concerns. What was said a minute ago is of particular importance to people of my generation, who lived their youth under a system where you had to denounce everything to the police. Therefore, it is repugnant to me as a lawyer, and also because I lived in France during the war, to be compelled to report things to the police. So, I always balance the necessity to fight against crime and this obligation.

QUESTIONS ON THE RISK OF PENAL LIABILITY

MARK PIETH *(translated from the French)*

I'd like to come back to the subject that was raised by the floor earlier. Indeed, you already have in France, today, the notion of liability for a legal entity. It's an objective standard: did the head of the company realize what was going on? If he did not, you have an issue as regards the intent to violate the law. Of course, someone who pays a bribe in Indonesia does so intentionally, it's only logical. But for the head of a French company, the issue is one of due diligence. This is a concept that already exists and is going to be adopted in other countries.

KRISTINE KARSTEN *(translated from the French)*

We lawyers spend a lot of time worrying about how to protect corporate officers and directors, knowing that they often have played no personal role in any wrongdoing. Usually, however, they are at least conscious that there is a risk that illegal activities will be conducted under their responsibility and in some cases they decide to close their eyes. There is a well-known case currently before the French courts, where a bank's officers, accused of facilitating money laundering, have offered as a defense the argument that they weren't aware of the problem and therefore could not have acted intentionally. Unfortunately, it would seem that they had asked their lawyer to look at the activities in question from a money laundering perspective and had already been advised that there was a risk that they could be characterized as money laundering. Did they then decide that it would cost too much to fix the problem? In any case, the prosecution seems to have implied intent from an informed assumption of risk.

How do you protect against this risk? A lot has been written on the subject, for example as regards delegations of authority. The idea here is, for example, that I, the President of the company, delegate authority to my Vice-President, who in turn delegates authority to the Sales Manager, who in turn delegates authority to his assistant, who maybe will delegate authority to the secretary who sends the memo authorizing payment of a bribe in Indonesia. Clearly, there are limits to the protection you can hope to obtain through delegations of authority.

ANTONIO CRIVELLARO *(translated from the French)*

I would like to make a suggestion. There was, in the past, a principle of international law called *crimina juris gentium*. You may remember it. What it covered was piracy, traditionally, then for a while the slave trade was considered to be a *juris gentium* crime, as were attacks by corsairs. In modern international law, air piracy is an interesting case: an international treaty was concluded very rapidly. Naturally, the international community wanted to eliminate these attacks, which are a tremendous obstacle to air communications. Even more modern is the case of drug trafficking and terrorism and, I would add, money laundering. I think that the modern legal community considers them to be *juris gentium* crimes.

MARK PIETH

I think it is a very important point, this concept of *crimina juris gentium*. There is a new concept that has superseded it, which is basically called macro criminality, with subsets of organised crime, corporate crime, state crime or what you might call para-state crime, which is terrorism and other forms of organised unrest.

It is very interesting that you very eloquently placed money laundering within this framework. But your reason was also very interesting, because it carries a high sentence. For me, it is interesting because I have been observing intimately the development of money laundering. I was involved with the Financial Action Task Force in 1989 for the first four years, where we were quite unsure what it was about. There, it was about drugs. As you say, those are serious crimes, drugs and money laundering.

In the meantime, money laundering is becoming an open umbrella concept affixed to any kind of predicate offence. You know the evolution: drugs, organised crime and then all serious crime. It is actually a very open concept that you can attach almost to anything, except perhaps to traffic offences.

Going on into corporate crime, you said fraud could be a macro crime. I would simply say that a lot of this could change. It is a matter of conceptualisation. What I would just like to draw your attention to is the question of bribery, certainly the question of large-scale bribery. You certainly have a point that there is a lot of small bribery which is not dangerous as such, but you also know that there is a lot of small theft and we still think that theft is a serious crime.

The problem is always that it is very difficult in legal concepts to make a distinction on the basis of the petty. That is where you have to distinguish between facilitation payments and others. My point is, really, you just have to wake up to the fact that as arbitrators you have legal obligations. You are also working within a legal context. My point is, according to Swiss law, if you are actually ordering the payment of something that would clearly be considered a bribe, as an arbitrator, you might be an accessory to bribery, because the crime is only finished when the bribe is paid under that construction. So, be careful.

SERGE LAZAREFF *(translated from the French)*
Coming back to the issue of money laundering, this is a problem where, as a matter of principle, bankers, companies and individuals are being called upon to participate in the effort to eliminate it. Corruption and like problems raise different issues. However much we may individually applaud, as a moral matter, the principle that corruption should be eliminated, you have to be realistic. You can sign treaties and participate in working groups. But what are the industrials going to do? They may die. If an arbitrator sees commissions of 10 or 15 %, he may say that smells of corruption and I

want nothing to do with it. But what if the commission is only 5 %? What we need to do, today, is to give some guidance to arbitrators who are responsible for resolving a dispute, who must issue a judgment, but who are not policemen and who are conscious that their decision may be catastrophic for the companies that are before them.

MARK PIETH

On your point about small or big amounts of bribery, I do not want to play the zealot here. I am very happy if grand corruption is covered. The difficulty is always if the law also covers cases that you do not really want it to.

Going back to my example of theft a moment ago, I am not a zero-tolerance person. I have no problem with shoplifting, frankly. But I think we all have a law against theft because we believe that it might go against the heart of the matter somewhere else. The difficulty is basically the same here. We are not talking about the petty payments. For instance, there can be a real difficulty for a country itself if this practice is endemic. If I have to stop at every corner to pay $10 here or $10 there to get something, that is a real problem for the country and the trust of the country in its own administration. That is not something that we can remedy from here. So, if you look at the North/South problem, it is not the North who can solve the South's problems. That is for the IFIs and for the countries themselves to solve.

But we can abstain from paying those $10 million, $100 million or $1 billion bribes. I have three cases which actually involve $1 billion. That is something that goes quite beyond anything that one can defend, I think.

QUESTIONS ON EVIDENCE

QUESTION FROM THE FLOOR

My question concerns another aspect of Mr. Jenkin's presentation, which is the tension that arises, in particular, in the case of arbitration, more so than the case in civil court proceedings, between a desire to obtain evidence for your client that is usable in an arbitration versus the desire to obtain evidence that is usable in a criminal proceeding. Particularly in arbitration, I have recently been seeing more and more cases where clients show up with evidence for which the chain of control of that evidence is not exactly clean, but which arbitrators just do not want to ask about as long as the evidence looks compelling. In an arbitration where there is a desire to move quickly towards a financial goal for your client, you have the desire to take this evidence and use it. In light of the particular obligations that are imposed on lawyers or on clients, how do you balance that obligation against the need to carefully gather evidence, perhaps with the use of experts, forensic experts, so that there is a chain of control established over the evidence, so that if you eventually see the need for a criminal action, the evidence can be turned over to authorities in a usable way?

ALAN JENKINS

My simple answer to that, and perhaps it is too simple, but that may be a function of the legal system in which I operate, is that I concern myself simply with what is required to prove my case before the arbitrators and I leave the police and the criminal prosecution service to look after themselves. That might be a little bit too simple, but it is, I think, a useful route map for a lawyer representing a client in civil proceedings, whether before a court or in an arbitration. His interest is in advancing his client's claim or defence in that arbitration, provided that what he does meets with the standards that the arbitrator would expect of a party appearing before him. He should not concern himself about whether the chain of control that you have described would be satisfactory to a criminal court.

That is, however, in a state of flux in the UK. It used to be the position that the courts were totally uninterested in how you came by the evidence and that goes back three or four hundred years. But as I mentioned in my presentation, we have just had a case in the commercial court in London in which the defendant argued that banking records had been obtained in breach of Swiss banking laws and the English Data Protection Act. The initial application was simply to obtain the report of the private investigators, which would normally have been protected by privilege of professional secrecy. The law reporters then pass in silence over what the judge actually did with the documents that he held should not be privileged. So, it is still uncertain how far this line is going to go. But for myself, and I think for every other English lawyer, we would not get involved in the dichotomy that you have described.

KRISTINE KARSTEN *(translated from the French)*

One further point might be made about evidence of money laundering. Under French law, for a start, there is today no need to prove that the underlying crime or offense was committed. The law says you must declare your suspicions when a transaction may have resulted from organized criminal activity. Full stop. Thus, for example, if you take the case of tax fraud, there is no need to prove that it actually occurred before attacking participants for money laundering.

COMMENT FROM THE FLOOR *(translated from the French)*

This issue is surrounded by uncertainties. I can understand, intellectually, that there should be no need to show that the underlying crime was committed when imposing an obligation to communicate your suspicions. But for a criminal prosecution for money laundering to succeed, surely you must show that the underlying crime occurred. Otherwise, you're expanding the notion of criminal responsibility in a manner that seems to me to be unreasonable. How can you base liability for money laundering on an objective standard without taking into account the notion of intent? The very expression, money laundering, implies that you are aware of what you are doing. It's like poisoning, which everyone agrees has to be intentional, or murder. I find it very imprudent for an assembly of jurists to take as a given that money laundering can be based on objective standards. There may be violations of ethical standards or professional errors or other sanctions without intent. But, particularly in light of the extension of the offenses underlying money laundering beyond drug trafficking and organized crime so that it can today be the outgrowth of any crime, it is particularly important to be vigilant concerning the circumstances under which an individual can be pursued for money laundering.

COMMENT FROM THE FLOOR *(translated from the French)*

I wonder whether we are not in danger of confusing issues concerning the degree of suspicion or wariness or doubt with issues arising under public law or penal law. Indeed, as we have seen, some countries make distinctions based on what you do: are you a lawyer protected by professional secrecy or are you a financial intermediary? We know that the distinction may be illusory, at least within the European Union. We also know that the degree of suspicion required before being obliged to report may vary from one country to the next in Europe. But these are matters of public law, whereas arbitration is a matter of private law. How can you say that an arbitrator sitting in one country has reporting obligations, or other obligations, that he would not have if he were sitting in another? And as regards the arbitral award, it is rare that you have proof that corruption or money laundering occurred. Instead, you can apply the traditional approach under private law, that is, that there will be a series of elements that will suffice to convince the arbitrator. The fact that, in England, a very slight suspicion means that you must report rapidly hopefully doesn't mean that this is the rule that will be applied when resolving private disputes. It is an obligation to the authorities only.

COMMENT FROM THE FLOOR *(translated from the French)*
I have a question concerning money laundering, because I have gathered from the discussion that there is a distinction being drawn between money laundering, on the one hand, and corruption, on the other, and that the panelists think that money laundering is extremely serious and should be punished in all cases, while corruption has to be looked at on a case-by-case basis and evaluated, notably, in light of the amounts at issue.

The reality, in the business world, is, it seems to me, a little different, in that the link between the litigious contract and the illegal act is more distant in the case of money laundering than it is in the case of corruption, where the contract itself is the vehicle for the corruption. In the case of money laundering, the contract serves to recycle the money that, originally, was the product of criminal activities. The link to the contract can be very distant.

The question is, what will come to the attention of the arbitrator? Is it reasonable to think, and this is an issue relating to proof and the arbitrator's power to obtain proof of criminal activities, such as drug trafficking, prostitution or other criminal endeavors, that the arbitrator can truly prove that these activities took place? Can the arbitrator truly go beyond mere suspicions? And if the arbitrator is limited to suspicions, should he declare his suspicions to the authorities and, if so, what are the implications for the proceedings being conducted before him? What should he do? I fail to see how an arbitrator, in practice, can prove that criminal activities that by definition have not been submitted to his review existed.

COMMENT FROM THE FLOOR

I think we all agree here that the thorniest issue is the problem of evidence. Whenever an arbitrator suspects that the transaction brought to his attention entails some sort of illegality, he has to exercise all the powers he has, which notoriously are far from being unlimited, to try to get enough evidence to determine that there is or there is not a situation of illegality. The process must stop at a certain point in time in terms of acquiring evidence. One mistake that has to be avoided is to mention in the award that the arbitrator suspected some illegality and that he was unable to find convincing evidence to support a conviction.

For example, a few years ago, a court of appeal in Trieste was requested to enforce an award, but refused the enforcement because the court found in the wording of the award the idea that the arbitrator had suspected some corruption, but was unable in the end to determine whether there was actually corruption. The court refused on the strength of Article 5-2 B, namely, in the name of Italian public order, the very idea of giving enforcement to an award which debated the subject whether or not there was corruption.

ARTHUR HARVERD

I think it would be very difficult for an arbitrator to find positively that there has been money laundering or some other wrongdoing because in order to determine that wrongdoing has been done, you need the enormous powers and resources of the state. It is extremely difficult to prove that there has been wrongdoing. There have been many cases before the courts where seemingly clear-cut position of guilt is apparent at the outset, but at the end of the trial, those who were charged have been found not guilty. And I wonder what the position would be if an arbitrator determined positively that there had been wrongdoing and six months down the line the individual was acquitted in the court. It does not seem to me that in the vast majority of arbitrations, the depth of evidence goes anywhere near what is required for a criminal court.

The only other observation I have made is that having worked with the police and other prosecuting authorities over many years on evidence of this nature, if someone gets reported to a prosecuting authority or police, nothing happens the next day. Life goes on as normal. In making a report or notification, it is not really such a serious matter that it will totally affect the individual that is being reported. The world does not collapse.

PROFESSOR SACERDOTTI

I just wanted to say that I believe the requirements of evidence in civil lawsuits are not the same at all as in a criminal lawsuit. I thus believe that it would be possible to determine with sufficient likelihood that there is, for example, money laundering in an arbitration even if it were not possible to prove criminal guilt.

QUESTIONS ON THE ROLE OF ARBITRATORS

KRISTINE KARSTEN *(translated from the French)*

We need to consider the role of arbitrators. When considering their duties, we might reflect on the duties of civil court judges in conventional state-run judicial systems. What are their obligations? Are they equipped or trained to identify suspicious activities? The primary difference between civil court judges and arbitrators is that an arbitrator is often a businessman familiar with complex transactions and perhaps better able to analyze them than ordinary civil judges, who are not necessarily, or even often, businessmen. Does an arbitrator have a greater responsibility because he is possibly more sophisticated in business matters?

COMMENT FROM THE FLOOR *(translated from the French)*

Fundamentally, what distinguishes an arbitrator from an ordinary judge? Today, we are asking arbitrators to be particularly vigilant. As soon as they become suspicious, they must make inquiries and, perhaps, file a report. Otherwise, they assume the risk that there was actually a fraud or other crime that they covered when rendering their award.

But how about the Taiwan frigates? You remember, the arbitrators deemed the contract valid and upheld it. There was an award and the contract was upheld. The matter went before the Swiss Federal Tribunal and the award was not set aside. But tomorrow, the arbitrators could be prosecuted. And the day after tomorrow, they could be condemned. The prosecutor may say, "My friends, you should have known. The commission was very large. You must have known. You go to prison." I mean here to be provocative.

Another problem we should address is that of the powers that arbitrators have. We have not looked at this. We have said that when there are questions, you should inquire, then make further inquiries. But what is the legal basis for this? Our reaction is natural, but once you have put your finger in the wringer, where do you stop? When you have a suspicion, when you make inquiries, what do you do if you don't get to the bottom of it? There is a point at which you need to stop. All I am saying is that we have opened, a little, Pandora's box.

COMMENT FROM THE FLOOR *(translated from the French)*

In Switzerland, for a long time, the legislation was relatively lax. Today, it is among the most stringent and effective in the world. But in the past, as an arbitrator, there were cases where you could legitimately suspect that you were in the presence of money laundering. There were two different situations that you might confront. The first was that where the parties were truly in dispute. In such a case, the position of the arbitrator was not fundamentally different from that of any other judge, that is to say, he had to make reasonable inquiries. The situation was much like that where corruption or another criminal offense was suspected.

The other case, however, is much more difficult for an arbitrator. It is that where the arbitrator suspects money laundering, but also suspects that the parties are actually in agreement and are using the arbitration as an expedient for obtaining a judgment of convenience in their simulated dispute. In this case, the arbitrator can request all the documents and proof he wants, but he can't be sure that he has received everything, or even that what he has received is not falsified. This is a problem for the arbitrator. On the more positive side, if the arbitrator is convinced that there is actually no dispute, its easier for him, because there is no reason for the arbitration to go forward. Why not let the parties settle their dispute privately, between themselves, in such a case? The solution is a contractual one, in such a case, not a judicial one. I see no reason for an arbitrator to hesitate to adopt this approach.

COMMENT FROM THE FLOOR *(translated from the French)*

If I take the example of an arbitration in which the parties file a request for arbitration, then file an answer, then fix the rules of arbitration, only to inform the arbitral tribunal, one month later, that they have negotiated a settlement that they would like the ICC to validate. There may be no submissions of proof on file, or very few. What is the arbitrator to do in a private dispute like this? Close his eyes and say, "Here's your award. It's yours. I'm not interested in what happened?" I don't think we can do that. We're not there to "rubber stamp" illicit transactions. What I do in cases like that is ask the parties to produce proof that the transaction was legitimate. If the parties refuse, I am entitled under the ICC Rules to refuse to validate the settlement through an award. No one obliges me to issue such an award. If the parties provide the proof, then I can issue the award. This is my approach.

PROFESSOR CRIVELLARO

If you look at ICC jurisprudence, as I have, it is clear that no case is the same as another. Naturally, the facts are very different from a case to the other. And facts influence arbitrators, tremendously and rightly so.

By way of example, look at the case that appears as no. 10 on my list. It is very interesting. The arbitrators asked the agent: "We take note that in your contract, it is expressly specified that you were acting on behalf of a 'group'. Could we ask you if you are in the position to specify how many members this group has and who are the other parties in this group?" No answer. Second question: "Why are you not in the position to answer?" Again, no answer. The arbitrators inferred that the failure to answer questions on the composition of the group meant something and so the decision went in a certain direction.

A second example is a case that was very well described by Bernardo Cremades in his written contribution. In that case, the first case he mentioned in his written paper, the respondent had refused to pay, but did not allege corruption. None of the parties even mentioned that word. It was an arbitrator who raised the suspicion. The majority said that the suspicion of an arbitrator, without having heard the parties on the matter, without having discussed the question, cannot be sufficient.

There is final case I would like to mention. A respondent refused payment on the basis that, in the question where the contract was to be performed, regulations had been enacted some days prior to the tender, prohibiting recourse to intermediaries. That prohibition did not exist when the agency agreement was signed. So, the respondent had cancelled the agreement with the agent. He thought that, given the regulations, he did not have to pay. The arbitrator held against him.

My last comment concerns the applicable law. I would take the liberty of repeating something that has been said this afternoon. Parties make an election of the law in their contract. I would point out, however, that the arbitrators are not always bound to follow the election made by the parties. That may be the law applicable to contractual obligations. But Article 7-1 of the Rules, if I am not mistaken, says that, in any case, the mandatory provisions of a law that is closely connected with the contract cannot be avoided. In many of these instances, the law of the importing country plays an important role and should be applied. And if it is to be applied, it helps the arbitrators much more than would questions of the administration of proof, which is sometimes, I agree, an impossible exercise. The answer is sometimes given by applying the law applicable in the importing country

COMMENT FROM THE FLOOR *(translated from the French)*
I go back to the distinction, with which I concur, between an arbitrator's obligations to report suspicions to the authorities and his duty to judge the matter before him. But there is a connection. If the arbitrator thinks he is obliged to declare his suspicions to the authorities, must he inform the authorities? Does he retain his ability to act as an impartial judge if he has reached this conclusion in the midst of the proceedings? I think this calls for some thought.

Look at the Lagergren decision. It was a decision on the merits, not a decision that the arbitral tribunal lacked competence to judge the matter. It's not the same as the decision made by the Pakistani High Court or the decisions reached under the former UK law. Competency is about dividing authority. There is always a court that is competent and, if it's not the arbitrator, then it's the state court. Lagergren says this quite clearly in the arbitral award: no tribunal, be it a state tribunal or an arbitral tribunal, can judge the matter. There is no grounds for suit. Arbitrators that fear they may be used to condone money laundering would do well to look at Lagergren.

BERNARDO CREMADES
We all suffer from an allergy to the duty to disclose. But as a lawyer or as an arbitrator, this duty is going to be imposed by the European Union legislation.

I think we should go back to the discussion as to what an arbitrator should do when a case of corruption, money laundering, or fraud comes before a tribunal. We cannot generalise. A contract of commission may be valid, but a contract of commission or agency may also entail massive corruption and it is up to the tribunal to go into that claim to hear the allegations of both parties. I do not think that this is a mistake. We as arbitrators, have no duty to sanction crime. That is not our position. Our position is very clear: we should react as an arbitrator and we should react by telling the parties, "Your allegations are either well founded or ill founded."

Then we come to the key question. We asked the arbitrators to be more proactive. That is clear. But how far should they be proactive? Due process is the limit and that is where the experienced arbitrator has to limit himself.

COMMENT FROM THE FLOOR

It has been indicated, with regard to suspicions under English law and also with regard to money laundering and the ICC directive, there is in fact a relationship with the authority of the arbitrator. If the arbitrator has the power to decide on money laundering issues, like any other matters, then it is of little consequence reporting it to the authorities. If the authorities have exclusive powers, then that may be a different question. But it would be contrary to the resolution of the International Law Association Commercial Arbitration Committee of Helsinki where we decided a few years ago that in a situation of fraud and criminal activity coming to the attention of an arbitral tribunal, the tribunal cannot suspend the proceedings, but must continue with the proceedings. This is one area.

Another, I believe, is that dealing with money laundering and similar issues is not an excess of power under the New York Convention or otherwise. We are entitled to deal with them when we feel that the issue is there. In many cases, adverse inference has been taken, unfortunately without prior notice to the parties, which is in principle a violation of due process.

But there are a number of ways of dealing with this issue, not necessarily by always deciding the main issue. In one case, concerning an international system control, president Briner dismissed a case for lack of jurisdiction on a different basis, not necessarily on the issue of the bribery of the former regime.

There are many issues of authenticity of documents, but a standard of proof, unfortunately, must at times be considered in the circumstances. You cannot always allow the fraudster to benefit by requiring a higher standard of proof from the victim. It depends on the relationship between the two parties, like the intermediary or a third party or a successor or shareholder or the new regime or the new directors in the company who have come and discovered what the former management has done. In that situation, you have to be more relaxed.

I noticed outside here something concerning circumstantial evidence in connection with the proof of bribery and corruption. In some circumstances that is an important aspect that we need to take into consideration. I remember I had a case in the ICC where the issue came up through the tribunal. It was not a matter of bribery, fortunately. It was a matter of whether or not the parties or one of them was violating tax or insurance laws or violating some other public policy laws where the parties, instead of allowing us to proceed with a consent award, wanted to withdraw the case and withdraw the case, not by the decision of the tribunal, but administratively through the ICC. I had some problems and so did my Chairman. Nonetheless, we considered that the ICC, if it agrees, has a practice on this. It can go ahead and let them withdraw the case.

There are various situations, I believe, of considerable significance and I would like to say that I have enjoyed your contributions.

Serge Lazareff

My own conclusion would be that we have witnessed today not a confrontation, but two different positions. The first one is the classic or liberal approach, which I must say is rather my own approach, even though we have observed today a very strong evolution. What is the classical approach? It is rather simple to me. It is that the jurisdiction of the arbitrator is clearly defined by the terms of reference or by the compromis.

If we might come back for a minute to the ICC Rules, and look at Article 18, you have the terms of reference. If you want to modify the terms of reference, you have to use Article 19. And then your role is defined.

I am rather surprised that I have never heard, not even once today, a reference to the concept of *pacta sunt servanda*. When you have two people who enter into an agency contract, they both know fully well what they are doing. Who is the victim? Is the situation that different from one where an arbitrator is faced with two parties, one of them being represented either by a poor lawyer or by someone not knowing how to argue? In such a case, we never dare say "that is the way you should argue". The maximum we are prepared to do, as Andrew Berkeley says, is to draw adverse inference if the party does not carry the burden of proof.

It seems to me that we are not far from a consensus, but it is a very subjective topic. I strongly believe that the arbitrator has more authority than he thinks he has. I believe that the arbitrator, as time goes by, is becoming closer and closer to the role and the authority of a state judge. But not yet. The arbitrator has a duty to fulfil his mission and render an award. That is what the rules say: "Once the arbitrator has accepted these duties, he must fulfil his mission."

There has been much discussion about Lagergren. I have a very simple question. What was he paid for? The parties have paid him to give an award. But what does he say? "No, no. I wash my hands." To me, this is a difficult position for an arbitrator. However, if you take the award by consent, then the Rules give you the authority to refuse an award by consent. That is in Article 26.

So what is my conclusion? First, yes, the arbitrator must be more pro-active. Certainly. He must look at evidence. But I do not think that he can go as far as some of you have stated or hinted today. Today, he owes his primary duty to the parties. He has been nominated or appointed by the parties for a certain purpose. He is not an agent of the state. Yes, he is a judge, but he is still a particular sort of judge. I suppose that in 10-20 years from now, he would have the same authority as a judge. But I think today, that is premature. I do not think the arbitrator should be put in this awkward position of being trusted by the parties and then either refusing an award or reporting the parties for something which, in his own opinion, is wrong. I think he would be going beyond his mission. This is my conviction.

We could go on for hours. But I think we should have a colloquium on one of these topics one of these days. Thank you all.

ICC at a glance

ICC is the world business organization. It is the only representative body that speaks with authority on behalf of enterprises from all sectors in every part of the world.

ICC's purpose is to promote an open international trade and investment system and the market economy worldwide. It makes rules that govern the conduct of business across-borders. It provides essential services, foremost among them the ICC International Court of Arbitration, the world's leading institution of its kind.

Within a year of the creation of the United Nations, ICC was granted consultative status at the highest level with the UN and its specialized agencies. Today ICC is the preferred partner of international and regional organizations whenever decisions have to be made on global issues of importance to business.

Business leaders and experts drawn from ICC membership establish the business stance on broad issues of trade and investment policy as well as on vital technical or sectoral subjects. These include financial services, information technologies, telecommunications, marketing ethics, the environment, transportation, competition law and intellectual property, among others.

ICC was founded in 1919 by a handful of far-sighted business leaders. Today it groups thousands of member companies and associations from over 130 countries. National committees in all major capitals co-ordinate with their membership to address the concerns of the business community and to put across to their governments the business views formulated by ICC.

Some ICC Services:
- ICC International Court of Arbitration (Paris)
- ICC International Centre for Expertise (Paris)
- ICC World Chambers Federation (Paris)
- ICC Institute of World Business Law (Paris)

- ICC Centre for Maritime Co-operation (London)
- ICC Commercial Crime Services (London), grouping:
  - The ICC Counterfeiting Intelligence Bureau
  - The ICC Commercial Crime Bureau
  - The ICC International Maritime Bureau

ICC Publishing S.A.

ICC Publishing, the publishing subsidiary of ICC, produces and sells the works of ICC commissions and experts as well as guides and corporate handbooks on a range of business topics. Some 100 titles – designed for anyone interested in international trade – are available from ICC Publishing.

For more detailed information on ICC publications and on the above-listed activities, and to receive the programme of ICC events, please contact ICC Headquarters in Paris or the ICC national committee in your country.

Selected ICC publications

E: English – F: French – D: German – S: Spanish – I: Italian – EF: bilingual

COMMERCIAL FRAUD AND COUNTERFEITING

Fighting Corruption

Fighting Corruption addresses key questions for managers concerning the prevention of extortion, bribery and other forms of corruption. How does a company develop a clear and enforceable code of conduct? What steps should it take to ensure that it is hiring qualified and reputable agents? How does one develop an accounting policy with explicit prohibitions against off-the-books or false entries? How does a company assess its vulnerability to money laundering and develop a know-your-customer policy? First published in 1999 as *Fighting Bribery*, this essential manual has been fully revised and updated with four new chapters – on extortion, whistleblowers, customs and small- and medium-sized enterprises. *Fighting Corruption* details concrete steps companies can take to protect themselves – and their shareholders – against unethical and unlawful acts by employees, external auditors and corporate officials.

E   244 pages   ISBN 92-842-1321-5   No. 652

Preventing Financial Instrument Fraud

This lively study by ICC Commercial Crime Services provides an invaluable reference manual and training aid for those in financial services, professionals and private investigators, and law enforcement agencies. Featuring a number of case studies that illustrate how criminals use documents to perpetrate a wide variety of very plausible scams, and how seriously the judiciary worldwide now treats this issue.

E   128 pages   ISBN 92-842-1217-7   No. 648

Trade Finance Fraud

You don't have to work long the business to realize that international trade is not just about buying and selling. It involves international transport, and that means putting cargoes in the hands of transport operators who are sometimes unscrupulous or under-capitalized. Traders and financiers need to be aware of what to do when this happens. Including case studies of some of the spectacular frauds that have resulted in recent dealings, this thorough and lucid text highlights the dangers and shows how traders and financiers can protect themselves, including an in-depth study of legal recourse.

E   84 pages   ISBN 92-842-1213-6   No. 643

Anti-Counterfeiting Technology Guide

A guide to protecting and authenticating products and documents
By ICC Commercial Crime Services, London
Written by the experts, this invaluable guide looks into the ever-present menace of counterfeiting and the various technologies that exist to distinguish originals from fraudulent copies, highlighting the key issues that need to be considered in selecting and using an appropriate technology. With the growing sophistication of counterfeiters, effective protection calls for the layering of different anti-counterfeiting technologies. This clear publication will provide expert guidance for those charged with product and document protection in a world where large-scale counterfeiters have become better resourced both in terms of finance and availability of technology and expertise.

E   80 pages   ISBN 92-842-1293-6   No. 630

Enforcement Measures against Counterfeiting and Piracy

By ICC Commercial Crime Services, London
An overview of the legal remedies and enforcement machinery available to fight counterfeiting and piracy in 31 key countries. Divided into two parts, the book explains the TRIPS agreement and presents information on anti-counterfeiting and anti-piracy measures in different jurisdictions. Full of carefully designed questions covering all the important aspects of enforcement of intellectual property rights, this survey provides a sound platform for the choice of the appropriate procedure in different countries.

E   212 pages   ISBN 92-842-1261-3   No. 608

Money Laundering

By ICC Commercial Crime Services, London
This guide explains how criminal revenue is made to appear legitimate and highlights the advantages of effective anti-money laundering administration procedures. Divided into three sections, it explains a framework for self-protection and provides case studies which illustrate the subject. The appendices outline business procedures, suspicious activity indicators, electronic cash (E-Cash) considerations, the Group of Seven Financial Action Task Force, financial institutions as defined by the US Bank Secrecy Act, and the Bank Secrecy Act regulations.

E   140 pages   ISBN 92-842-1243-X   No. 585

Countering Counterfeiting

By ICC Commercial Crime Services, London
A concise practical manual describing the nature, scale and impact of product counterfeiting and outlining strategies that can be adopted to prevent it and protect against it. The guide describes ways in which victims of counterfeiters can respond through the protection and enforcement of their intellectual property rights.

E   120 pages   ISBN 92-842-1231-X   No. 574

INTERNATIONAL ARBITRATION

Collection of ICC Arbitral Awards, Vol IV (1996-2000)

By Jean-Jacques Arnaldez, Yves Derains, Dominique Hascher
The latest *Collection of ICC Arbitral Awards* contains extracts of cases handled by the ICC Court of Arbitration, with indexes from preceding volumes dating back to 1974. It contains a consolidated analytical table, in both English and French, with extensive cross-references based on the terminology used in awards and case notes; a chronological index listing the awards and contains references to legal literature; a key word index, also provided in both languages, allowing the reader to locate the material of interest quickly and easily; and a cross-referenced index of cases referring to the J*ournal du droit international*, the *Yearbook Commercial Arbitration* and the *International Construction Law Review* for each of the awards published in the *Collection.* Co-published with Kluwer International.

EF   850 pages   ISBN 92-842-0316-3   No. 647

ICC International Court of Arbitration Bulletin

The *ICC International Court of Arbitration Bulletin* contains information and comment of practical relevance to businesses and their lawyers contemplating or already involved in ICC arbitration proceedings, plus the 2002 statistical report on ICC dispute resolution services.
Available by subscription. For further information, visit **www.iccbooks.com**.

E-F   88 pages

International Chamber of Commerce Arbitration (3rd edition)

By W. Laurence Craig, William W Park, Jan Paulson
This classic reference book is essential reading for anyone involved in an ICC arbitration. With its practical approach and step-by-step analysis, the updated text takes into account the 1998 revision of the Rules and includes fully updated statistics and interesting recent cases. Co-published with Oceana.

E   952 pages   ISBN 92-842-1251-0   No. 594

INTERNATIONAL TRADE

A to Z of International Trade

By Frank Reynolds

More than a dictionary, *A to Z* doubles as a reference book, developing terms in context and showing how they interact. Including over 2000 definitions and acronyms as well as website addresses, the dictionary's thorough cross referencing system enables you to define a word from start to finish. And *A to Z* takes you further, with its nine "Focus on" sections, providing well-researched introductions on air transport, bank collections, e-commerce, Incoterms, insurance, letters of credit, sales contracts, liner vessel shipping and vessel chartering. *A to Z* really helps you understand the language of international trade.

E   343 pages   ISBN 92-842-1277-4   No. 623

Guide to Export-Import Basics (2nd edition)

A fully revised edition of this ICC bestseller. Providing clear explanations of the core mechanics of trade, this guide takes a lucid look at the legal, financial, transport and e-commerce issues. Fully indexed, it also includes a handy glossary of the principal terms and abbreviations.

E   360 pages   ISBN 92-842-1309-6   No. 641

Key Words in International Trade (4th edition)

Over 3000 translations of the terms and abbreviations most commonly used in international law and commerce, taken from the fields of banking, transport, management, marketing, arbitration, trade, telecommunications and international organizations.

EFSDI   408 pages   ISBN 92-842-1187-5   No. 417